IN MY NATURE:

A BIRDER'S YEAR AT THE MONTLAKE FILL

BY CONSTANCE SIDLES

Illustrations by Alexandra MacKenzie

Constancy Press, LLC   Seattle, Washington

In My Nature: A Birder's Year at the Montlake Fill
First Edition

Copyright © 2009 Constancy Press, LLC

Published and distributed by Constancy Press, LLC
4532 48th Avenue NE
Seattle, WA 98105 USA
phone: (206)522-7513
http://www.constancypress.com

Printed in Hong Kong by Mantec Production Company
September 2009

ISBN: 978-0-9842002-0-7 $19.95

Library of Congress Control Number: 2009907929

Dedication and Acknowledgements

Just as the Montlake Fill itself did not come into being through the efforts of a single individual, neither does a book like this. It takes the efforts of an entire community. In fact, if I counted up all the people who contributed to this book—a kind of life list of helpers, as it were—it would be almost as long as my life list of birds at the Fill.

There are some special people who stand out, though, and whom I would like to thank. First is my husband, John, who let me drag him out to bird at all hours in all weathers, who told me every day, "You are a great birder and a great writer," whether I am or not, and who labored long and hard to learn the mark-up language that made this book come to life on press.

Next are my three kids, who patiently listened when I needed to talk and talked when I needed to listen.

Next is my dear friend and colleague, Alex MacKenzie, who helped make my stories vivid with her beautiful paintings. Also on my list are Nick Allison, who edited my work in the kindest yet most rigorous fashion and who is among the best editors on the planet; and Amy Davis, a dear friend who waded through the whole text to find every last typo and grammatical error.

To them and to the dozens of birders and photographers in our community who shared their birds, their art, and their thoughts with me every single day, thank you. To Rolfe Kellor, Sedge Thomson, and Neal Lessenger, who helped me with the history of the Fill, you were a gold mine of information, kindness, and support. To Kern Ewing, Fred Hoyt, Doug Schmitt, and all the other staff of the CUH who have worked so hard to keep the Fill wild and natural, you're the greatest. And to my mentor, Dennis Paulson, who generously taught me about the birds in our state and who encouraged me to give back to our birding community:

This book is dedicated to all of you.

Contents

Illustrations & Photographs

Part I
Winter

1. In the Beginning

"Do we have to hit every pothole?" I asked my husband. "My fillings are going to fall out."

"Keep your eyes down," he cautioned, staring intently into the blackness of the road. "It's starting to get light."

"Hurry."

We were going the speed limit already—15 mph—on the pitted gravel road leading into the Dime Lot on the University of Washington campus. It was predawn, January 1, and we were on a quest to see our First Bird of the Year at my favorite place on Earth, the Montlake Fill.

The Fill, officially known as the Union Bay Natural Area, is 75 acres of rolling hills, riparian woods, lake edge, ponds, and cultivated gardens located just north of Union Bay on Lake Washington. It is a former landfill—now a natural area—in the heart of Seattle, used by more than 240 different species of birds.

My husband John and I had argued for days about the best strategy for finding a "good" bird to be number one. There were plenty of possibilities, but there were also some possible duds. High on my dud list were crows.

American Crows are so abundant at the Fill that sometimes they cover the sky like an ebony featherbed flung up by an invisible Earth Mother covering her child. Crows have their diehard fans, but I am not one of them. Every time I see a crow, I am reminded of President John F. Kennedy's farewell address to the Commonwealth of Massachusetts, which he delivered just before he left the state to assume the presidency: "For of those to whom much is given, much is required."

Crows are among the brainiest of all birds, but what do they use their brains for? To pry open my garbage can, extract garbage, and spread it all over the block. To peck other birds who aren't doing a thing to them. To gather in their thousands on the asphalt parking lot north of Husky Stadium and malevolently eye innocent passersby.

No, First Bird of the Year should not be a crow.

Neither should it be a starling. European Starlings are also abundant at the Fill. In the winter, they gather in huge bird-balls that bounce around the sky. Starlings are smart, adaptable birds with iridescent feathers and bright yellow bills—eye-catching—but they are not native. They were introduced to this country from England by Eugene Schieffelein in 1890 and 1891. Schieffelein was a member of the American Acclimation Society. Acclimation societies, a popular movement in the nineteenth century, were formed to introduce Old World species of plants and animals to the New World in a kind of "*mi casa es su casa*" attempt to bring the world closer together.

Schieffelein's group decided to introduce all the birds mentioned in Shakespeare. The 60 starlings they released in New York have now multiplied into more than 200 million birds blanketing the nation. As did so many other immigrants, a hefty proportion of starlings decided that Seattle is the place to be. I knew that starlings would be high on my year list—that was inevitable—but I didn't want them to be number one.

Our best chance to avoid both crows and starlings, we decided, was the south end of the Dime Lot. This area butts up against a slough on the west, a lagoon on the south, and a pond on the east. With all that water nearby, we figured our chances of seeing a shorebird, waterfowl, or wader at dawn would be high.

We pulled into the parking lot and got out cautiously. Still too dark for crows or starlings, thank goodness. I headed for the lagoon, while John chose the slough. As we thrashed about in the darkness, making enough noise to frighten off any self-respecting bird, John spotted something. "Psst, over here," he hissed. But I was stuck in the brambles that guard the lagoon as thickly as the thorn forest around Sleeping Beauty's castle. "Over here, quiiiiick," my husband insisted. "It's a Great Blue Heron." The official bird of the City of Seattle. A great start to the year.

I might as well have been set in concrete. I couldn't move.

In desperation, I yoinked my legs out of the blackberries' grip, gouging bloody troughs right through my pants, but it was too late. The heron had flown off, disappearing into the night without a trace. In its place was an American Wigeon, perhaps the dumbest duck in creation. Ducks, on the whole, are not avifauna's Einsteins, but wigeons are dim even for ducks. In nineteenth-century England, wigeon was a synonym for "dumb cluck."

Somehow, it seemed appropriate that the First Bird of the Year for me would be a wigeon. The New Year is a time to begin new things, and every beginner knows you can't be afraid to look stupid. Since I'm a great believer in trying new things, I frequently experience the discomfort of feeling like a dumb cluck.

But there was another reason why a wigeon was a good bird to start off the year. American Wigeons are an everyday bird at the Fill in winter. There are thousands dabbling on Lake Washington. Every night, they fly in to roost on the ponds that dot the Fill. I have often sat under the Lone Pine Tree above Shoveler's Pond at dusk and listened while wigeons by the dozen fly in. Their feathers whistle as they glide by, and their cries sound like a carousel organ that can play only three notes: tew-TEW-tew. It is a magical experience, and that is my point. A thing does not have to be rare to be wonderful.

I learned this lesson from my husband, who has a great antipathy for celebrations. Birthdays, anniversaries, holidays, festivals—he dislikes them all. On those special occasions when everyone else on the planet would give his wife a bouquet of flowers, John gives me a homily. He says that every day should be a special day—we shouldn't have to wait for one to come around on a given date.

It took me years to understand that he wasn't just trying to get out of a shopping expedition. In fact, I can identify the date when I finally began to understand. It was 2003. That was the year when

all three of my children were gone from home. One was fighting a war in Iraq. One was attending college in Chicago. One was living in Ukraine, visiting family for a year. The worry, loneliness, and emptiness in my life were almost unbearable. I tried to fill my days with work and with birding. Weekends were the hardest because neither John nor I could use our jobs as distractions. To get away from the silence at home, we spent nearly every weekend on the road, looking for birds in some corner of the state.

Eventually as the years passed, the kids began to straggle back home now and then to visit or to stay a while. I came to realize how grateful I was for their appearances. When my youngest son moved back to his own apartment here in town, he would stop by our house unannounced once or twice a week. Sometimes I wasn't home, but I always knew when he had come around because the toilet seat would be up and my bananas would be gone. I learned to treasure the times when I knew that he had breathed the same air as I, walked on the same carpet, slammed shut the same front door. Little pleasures like that began to loom larger and larger for me, until now they dominate my life.

I now know that the best-lived life is filled with small things that seem small only if we fail to recognize how much they really do matter to us:

The day my husband came home from work, made straight for the bedroom to change out of his professor costume, I heard his shoes go clunk! in the closet, and we both realized that 30 years of nagging had finally paid off. Yes, he crowed, he *did* learn to put his shoes where they belong. Then he and I both stared at my own shoes that I had left to languish beside the sofa. Evidently, I'm the one who needs nagging. How we both laughed.

The bread I baked with my daughter, the perfect loaves turning brown in the oven, and the crowbar we needed to pry the loaves off the baking sheet because they somehow got welded onto the metal. We never figured out how.

The sock I rolled onto my friend's foot because she had just had hip surgery and wasn't supposed to bend.

It is in these common, everyday events where I seek my greatest enjoyment, and it is there that I invariably find happiness.

Dennis Paulson, one of our state's best and most generous ornithologists, knows this, too. Periodically, Paulson teaches a master birding class for the Seattle Audubon Society. One day, he gave our class an assignment. We were to go to our favorite birding spot, find any bird we chose, and try to follow that bird for a day, writing down everything the bird did.

I chose to go to the Fill and follow an American Wigeon, on the theory that I had a pretty good chance of finding one that would hang around all day. Sure enough, on the Main Pond I easily found a sleeping wigeon. I set down my camp stool, hauled out a notebook, and began to record the bird's activities. I decided I would write down a notation once every five minutes. I filled the first page with the same observation, written again and again: "Bird asleep." "Bird still sleeping." "Bird taking a long snooze." I started on the second page, wondering if the bird was really dead and just hadn't fallen over yet. But then it woke up and began to preen.

I was thrilled because I had never before paid close attention to this activity, and now—thanks to Dennis's assignment—here was my chance. From books, I knew that each feather has vanes that grow out of a central shaft. The vanes are made up of parallel branches. From each branch grow tiny branchlets, called barbules, with hooks on the ends. The hooks fasten the barbules together like Velcro, creating a very strong but light structure. Birds must give regular maintenance to their feathers, oiling them from a gland at the base of their tails and re-hooking the barbules together. But just exactly how do they go about it?

In the case of my wigeon, it started on its left wing, advanced to the breast feathers, and then attacked its right flank. I began to wonder if there was any method to the wigeon's work. After all, a wigeon has thousands of feathers—how does it know which ones to focus on? Do neglected feathers give off some kind of a signal, such as an itch? Or does the duck remember where it left off the last time it preened? Does it preen all the feathers in one day, or does it take several days to do the whole bird? Are some feathers more important than others? Do they get preened more often, or are all the feathers on the same maintenance schedule? Are all birds as assiduous as my wigeon, or are there lazy ones who can't be bothered, just as there are people who don't floss their teeth every day?

The more I watched, the more entranced I became. About 30 minutes into its preening, the wigeon looked up, gave a little "tew," and then flew off, leaving me to marvel and wonder. An ordinary duck? I never thought so again. An ordinary day, an ordinary life? There is no such thing.

Back at the Fill on January 1, I watched the pale dawn light up my First Bird of the Year as it floated peacefully on the slough. The iridescent green of the wigeon's head gleamed like the world's most whopping emerald. I lowered my binoculars, completely happy. "Let's go find a crow," I said to my husband. He smiled.

2. Mallards

In a Seattle winter, nobody dreams of a white Christmas. We contend more with gray skies and rain than we do with ice and snow. But every now and then, a cold blast arrives from the Arctic, and Seattle enters a deep freeze.

During such winters, the Fill becomes unworldly. Snow muffles the few sounds of city traffic—most people know to stay safely home. Birds have no such option, however. They must stay out in all weathers and endure as best they can.

Which is why on one particularly arctic morning, with the air blazingly clear and snow still on the ground, I set out to find birds at the Fill. It's always fun to find wild nature in the heart of a major city, but it's even more fun when the city must retreat into the background, allowing the wild to come forth.

My first stop was the Main Pond, my target the Mallards. Male Mallards begin their breeding season in the fall, when they molt out of their camouflaged "eclipse" plumage and put on the gemstone greens, blacks, purples, whites, and browns that they hope will attract a mate. Mallards, unlike geese or swans, pair up for only one season. Once the pair have accomplished their goal of mating, the male leaves the female alone to raise her young. While she toils at the nest and then later with her brood, the male works hard at getting rid of his conspicuous breeding plumage so he can better blend in with the background and evade predators.

Of course, once the female has finished her parenting and is ready for another batch of young, the males have to be prepared to court her. The male that is geared up the soonest has an advantage. So over the millennia, male Mallards have evolved a rather short eclipse period. By the time winter arrives, they are as bright as newly polished jewels.

On this snowy day, I thought the Mallards' green heads would look very fine against the white backdrop of the rolling hills of the Fill. Sure enough, a few males in breeding plumage were standing on the ice that covered the Main Pond, their orange legs bright as the sunrise. A little to the north, a small patch of open water had resisted the temptation to freeze solid. As I watched, the males on the ice lifted their eyes skyward and began to quack. Another male was flying in for a landing. He lowered his orange feet as Mallards always do, but then instead of skimming along the water to a graceful halt, he hit the ice and began to spin. He couldn't stop or steer, no matter how much he flailed his wings. Inexorably, he shot toward the hole in the ice, until, with a wild-eyed "Quack," he skated sideways off the edge and into the water, where he disappeared with a mighty splash. When he popped up again, the other ducks wouldn't look at him. He wiggled his tail nonchalantly, as if he had always meant to end up in the water, but we all knew different. I guess he was as inexperienced with the icy conditions as any other Seattleite.

When the excitement died down and all the ducks became still again, I began to wonder how the other males could endure standing on the ice. Why weren't their feet freezing solid? But then I remembered my final exam in college biology. We had studied the building blocks of life all year long, but on the final exam, the professors decided we should apply our theoretical knowledge to the real world. One of their most diabolical questions was: Why don't ducks' feet get cold in the water?

Never having imagined that my college biology course was supposed to have anything to do with the real world, my mind went blank. I had no clue.

The answer, as I learned when I got my awful test results back, turned out to be heat exchange. Ducks have a special arrangement of blood vessels in their legs and feet. The veins and arteries there lie close together so that warm blood from the heart can pass by cooled blood in the veins. Because the two vessels exchange heat, the ducks' feet stay warm. It was gratifying to see that the system worked well, even when the water was frozen.

The Fill is a convention center for ducks in the winter. Out on the open water of Lake Washington, Mallards are joined by their cousins the Gadwalls, as well as Wood Ducks, Green-winged Teals, Northern Shovelers, Buffleheads, Greater and Lesser Scaup, Ring-necked Ducks, Canvasbacks, Common and Hooded Mergansers, Ruddy Ducks, and American Wigeons. Among the huge rafts of American Wigeons, with their distinctive cream-striped green heads, I always look for the rare Eurasian Wigeon, a Siberian relative whose head is a glowing chestnut.

It is said that in Western Washington in the winter, you should be able to see one Eurasian Wigeon for every hundred American Wigeons. This number is an estimate, of course, but on this day, statistics didn't lie. One Eurasian Wigeon was swimming in the bay. I discovered this thanks to the UW crew, who were out rowing their eight-man shells on the lake, and thanks to their coach, who decided that a little yelling might provide some motivation. The wigeon flock, you see, was far out in the middle of the lake, too far for me to make them out as more than little black specks. Luckily, the ducks were right in the path of the rowing crew and the coach who followed them in a motorboat, his megaphone clamped to his mouth as though he had welded it there.

The coach reminded me of the galley master in the movie *Ben-Hur*, whose job it was to beat out the rhythm for the slaves working the oars (boom…boom…boom…boom). At one point, the captain needed to ram another ship. "Ramming speed!" cried the galley master, and boomboomboomboomboom, the ship shot forward. In the same way, "Ramming speed!" cried the coach (or something similar) and the students' shells shot forward, causing all the ducks on the bay to scatter in fright and settle much closer to shore.

After glassing through the now visible flock, I found one Eurasian Wigeon paddling nearby, his chestnut head almost afire in the bright sunlight. I had a feeling that he has been here all winter but too far out on the lake to be spotted. His rosy chest feathers were a beautiful contrast to the natty gray-and-black worsted of his flanks, like a staid businessman who sports a tie just bright enough to catch the eye and set him apart from his dumpier colleagues. Seeing this visitor from Siberia was simply stunning, and I owed it all to a grumpy coach with a big megaphone. I highly recommend going birding around 4:00 p.m., when the crew coach is at his testiest.

I don't know why exactly, but it always gives me unusual pleasure to see a rare bird. I think it's because I feel so much satisfaction in knowing that nature still harbors a diversity of species. Despite the precipitous drop in numbers of individual birds of many different species, Earth still is home to great diversity.

This is a reason to celebrate. Every species, you see, has been slowly adapting itself over thousands, if not millions, of years, honing its genome to take advantage of its own special niche in finding food, shelter, and mates. Each species, therefore, is the product of huge, sustained effort. It's almost as though a painter had taken a million years to paint one portrait, perhaps laying down only one brush stroke every century.

How rare and precious and wonderful would be that portrait.

And so, when I can count as many as fifteen different species of ducks in one day at the Fill, and up to 50 species of birds, I feel the glory of nature and all it took to get to this one point, on this one day, when the Mallards' heads gleam like emeralds and one lone Eurasian Wigeon dabbles blithely on the lake.

3. Crows

According to Native American legend, Raven and Crow, though outwardly similar in appearance, were very different in their outlook on life. Raven was a creator spirit. Although he was often a trickster, he could be nice if he chose. His favorite thing to do was to loose new things into the world, but he seldom did so for purely altruistic reasons. A typical Haida legend, for example, says that Raven created people simply because he was bored being alone. One day, when Raven was walking along the beach, he heard mysterious squeaks coming out of a clamshell. He pried it open and found creatures of a whole new species inside. Raven coaxed them out. That's how humans entered this world.

Crow, on the other hand, was more sinister than Raven, not a trickster but rather a seeker after his own welfare. Raven could sometimes be mean; Crow nearly always was. The Kiowas, for example, tell of a time when Crow was a white bird who used to warn all the buffalo when the hunters were coming, so the hunters never caught a thing. Not that Crow cared about helping the buffalo. He only wanted to deprive the other People. To ensure that he himself never went without, Crow kept a few buffalo for himself in a hole under his lodge. But the other People starved.

Pure meanness.

Coyote noticed that Crow was not losing weight the way everyone else was. Crow stayed fat. Coyote suspected that Crow was hiding his own food and selfishly denying it to everyone else. The wily Coyote thought of a way to find out. He told Owl and Dragonfly to watch Crow carefully. The two did their jobs so well that

Owl's eyes got big and Dragonfly's eyes bugged out. They saw Crow hiding his own stash of buffalo while telling the other buffalo when the hunters were coming to hunt them.

When Owl and Dragonfly told the other People about this act of selfishness, the People caught Crow and smoked him over a fire until he turned completely black. Then they let him go. Coyote decreed that from then on, Crow would be allowed to eat only scraps. That's why even today crows are avifauna's best and most persistent Dumpster divers.

This recognition of Crow as Bad Bird came to mind one winter day at the Fill when I discovered that several thousand crows had decided to make two fields into a roost. Crows littered the grass from the lake all the way up to Wahkiakum Lane—two solid acres of crows. Some were waddling along, clacking at each other like politicians working a crowd. Others were looking for the last hapless insect that had so far survived the cold but stood no chance against thousands of sharp eyes.

Those eyes focused on me warily as I walked along the trail. Each crow gave me a wide berth as I approached, but each gave me a good look, too. Their eyes glittered. What thoughts lay behind their alien sparkle? How hungry were they, anyway? The crows' scrutiny was unnerving. There were so many of them. If birds are indeed descendants of the dinosaurs, then crows must have come from *Tyrannosaurus rex*.

The thought occurred to me that it would be bad if crows ever got the idea of working together. They could easily annihilate me. As I speculated about the possibility, a faint choppa-choppa sound drifted over the ridge to the south. It was a helicopter coming in to land at the helipad west of the Fill.

The crows did not like the sound. They became agitated. Their clacking increased. Their eyes began to shift wildly, their heads to bob. When the helicopter finally appeared, the crows' agitation boiled over. In one massive sheet, they rose up into the air, as though someone had shaken open a black shroud. They began to circle the Fill in a giant, cawing swirl. Round and round they flew, growing angrier by the second. The sky was black with them from horizon to horizon. Every few seconds, a crow would break out of the shroud and fly at me, its open beak emitting cries of fury. I fled.

Artists from Herman Melville to Alfred Hitchcock have created frightening images of animals that have cracked under the pressure of humankind's unkindness toward them. Revenge is sweet, say these artists. See what it feels like to be prey?

Over the millennia, we have lost that feeling of being prey. No longer wary, no more imbued with the need for situational awareness, we have climbed to the top of the food chain, lords of the Earth and all who live here. Oh, there may still be the odd scrap of nature here and there that eludes our dominance for now—pesky viruses, bacteria, or cockroaches—but we know it's only a matter of time and technology before we control those things as well.

In our arrogance, we remake our ecology every day, and not often with ecology in mind. On my block, for example, little houses are rapidly being bulldozed into a mere memory, to be replaced by enormous boxes of controlled habitat, filled with entertainment centers, kitchens more suitable to four-star restaurants, and sun rooms that let in the sun but keep out the planet. Why need we bother to ever go outside again?

But critters perched at the top of the food pyramid should remember that the top is a small place. It's easy to lose your balance and fall off. Top predators of all other species but ours are few in number because they live in balance with their prey. The balance can be easily upset.

We think that we have turned these truths on their heads, that we can continue to rule nature without limiting our use of resources. Maybe so. But also maybe someday, the crows will decide it's time to band together and do what Alfred Hitchcock and the Kiowa believed crows will always do: seek new sources of food scraps. If that day ever arrives, I hope I'm not at the Fill.

A few weeks after my experience, my husband rode his bike through the Fill to work. His route took him along Wahkiakum Lane and over the New Wooden Bridge to the paved parking lot

that stretches for hundreds of meters on the western boundary of the Fill. On this morning, the parking lot was stacked solid with crows. Apparently, the 10,000 had decided that pavement warmed by the previous day's sun was preferable to cold, dewy grass fields, so they had set up their roost in the parking lot.

From one end of the lot to the other, John saw nothing but crow bodies, some with heads tucked in for sleep, others pacing restlessly, jostling their fellows. As he braked his bicycle to a stop and dismounted, the crows became aware of him. Their heads came up, their eyes stabbed him, and they froze.

John stared back. A standoff. Then he noticed a lone car parked in the middle of all the crows. Apparently, the driver had seen him, too. She rolled down her window. "Can you help me, please?" she quavered. "I'm too afraid to get out of my car."

Wheeling his bike slowly through the sea of crows, which broke apart before him as though he were a one-man icebreaker, my husband reached her car. The woman got out, and the two of them began walking toward the exit. The crows made no sound as they sidled away from the pair. They made no overt sign of threat. But they watched, their beady, unreadable eyes stuck to the interlopers.

When my husband and the woman reached the far side of the parking lot, they both breathed a sigh of relief. John said it was the last time he would ever do that again.

"I guess I'm just weak meat," he laughed. But it was a thin laugh, the kind a man might make who's realized just how much edible protein he really is packing around on his bicycle.

4. You Say Tomato,
I Say Tomahto

When you visit the Fill as often as I do, you eventually become a known character of the neighborhood. People who take their morning constitutional every day at the same time start saying hello. The couple who walk their two Giant Schnauzers every day (and who look a bit like them) give me a nod of recognition when they march by. Even the middle-aged jogger who sounds like an expiring steam locomotive as he puffs his way for the third time around the Loop Trail gives me a smile when he passes me. To be sure, it's only a brief rictus disturbing the rigidity of his features—he doesn't want to lose the intensity of his focus—but for me, he will break concentration for all of two seconds. We're friends, of a sort. Familiars, anyway.

Every now and then, one of the regulars will stop and ask me a bird question. The most common question I get is, "What's the name of that bird I saw?"

Their question is almost never asked at the moment when my interlocutors actually see the bird. On the contrary, the bird in question is almost always one they saw several days ago. They go into lengthy descriptions of size, color, and shape, but nothing in their accounts ever sounds remotely familiar. For all I know, the bird they saw could have been anything from a robin to a roadrunner. But people persist. Even in the teeth of my utter cluelessness, they want me to Name That Bird. So eventually I do. "Sounds like a Red-breasted

Sapsucker to me," I'll say, or, "Must have been a Chipping Sparrow." "Could have been a Nashville Warbler." "Starling, maybe."

It doesn't really matter what I say. Once I have "identified" the bird, the people smile and go on their way. In reality, they know nothing more than they did before they accosted me. After all, I never saw their bird, so how can I identify it for sure? Nevertheless, there is something about giving their bird a name that is deeply satisfying to folks.

I first encountered the all-importance of names when I was an Egyptology student at the University of Chicago. There, I learned that names have power. They confer immortality.

The ancient Egyptians certainly believed this, and they should know. They took their immortal afterlife very seriously. They wanted to be sure that they would have a comfortable one. So before they died, they spent a lot of effort accumulating goods that were to be buried with them, a kind of hope chest for eternity, as it were. Food, drink, clothing, pets, sports equipment, cosmetics—they packed for a long stay.

We look indulgently at these ancient beliefs now. "Oh, those naïve people," we say with a chuckle, "don't they know you can't take it with you?"

Actually, the ancient Egyptians did worry about that. They were very well aware that tomb robbers rifled even the best-hidden graves. To guard against this, the Egyptians painted pictures of their goods on the tomb walls. The idea was that since they were dealing with spirits anyway, not flesh and blood, representations of their stuff would probably be okay. But as any father of a budding artist knows, "You can't eat art." Oh, those naïve Egyptians.

Well, maybe not. The ancient Egyptians subscribed to the notion that nothing is certain in life except death and taxes, so they knew that even paintings might not suffice. Eternity is a very long time, even to people who build pyramids. To cover their bets, the Egyptians did one more thing before they embarked on their journey to the netherworld: they always tried to include in their tombs the name of the deceased written on some document, be it a wall painting, a small artifact, an obelisk, or even a potsherd. They had a saying: "He lives forever whose name is spoken." They hoped that someday, perhaps far in the future, someone might find their name and read it out loud, thus bringing the owner back to life, at least in the spirit world.

This is anything but a naïve concept, for isn't it true that a person is immortal whose accomplishments live on after death, or whose memory is kept alive by those who were influenced by that person? And isn't it true that we bring those memories and events to life by naming that person?

History is filled with examples. We still benefit from the wisdom of the Founding Fathers who created our Constitution. When we argue about a point of constitutional law, our judges refer to what Thomas Jefferson must have meant, or James Madison, or Alexander Hamilton. Praxiteles was supposedly the most skilled sculptor who ever lived in ancient Greece, yet only one of his statues survives, and that one may not even be his. His reputation is based mainly on the praise heaped upon him by ancient Greek and Roman admirers who wrote about his work. His name lives, and in a sense, so does he.

In a less exalted way, we carry with us the memories of our loved ones who no longer walk the Earth with us but who live on because we say their names, and this allows us to remember their lives. My mother lives on in me. I know this is true because when I speak her name, I can hear her voice in my mind. That voice comes out eerily when I find myself channeling her spirit to my kids. "Button up when you go out the door." "Breakfast is the most important meal of the day." "Chicken noodle soup will cure almost every disease."

It is the saying of names that evokes the immortal spirits because a name represents the person. It is a metaphor for everything that person was, did, said, believed, felt.

In fact, language itself is a metaphor. We see this when we try to teach robots to talk. Robots have a hard time with metaphor. They don't get it. They try to get at it by using one of their strengths—huge memory—to assemble every known example of a given word, find the commonalities, and then generalize. Take the word "building," for example. What is a building? Well, a building is something people have built, but not just that. People build lots of things that are not buildings: cars, model airplanes, relationships. A building is something that people have built and that they occupy, but not just that. People build tents and occupy them, yet tents are not buildings. True buildings have some permanence.

Beyond that, though, it's hard to say what it is that buildings all have in common.There are so many different kinds of buildings: pyramids, skyscrapers, towers, castles, huts, stadiums, natatoriums, bathhouses, theaters, churches, parliaments, sheds, houses, hotels. Some are tall, some are short, some smooth, some rough. Most have straight edges, whether they're rectangular or cylindrical, but there used to be a building downtown that had no straight edges at all. People called it the Blob. The list of everything that qualifies as a building is long and complicated. Oh, the poor robot.

People have none of these difficulties. Babies learn what a building is before they're two years old. They learn their native language before they enter kindergarten. Somehow, people know what all their words symbolize. They know the nuances that different words represent. They know that rage is different from anger. Love can be passion, but it can also be compassion. A tree is a kind of plant and so is a ranunculus, but a tree is not a blossom.

Birds have nothing like this. They do have songs and calls that communicate ideas, but the ideas are pretty simple and very direct. "Lookin' good; come on over and mate with me," a male might sing. Or, "Yikes, a falcon! Everybody up in the air, quick!" Or, "Yum, tasty McDonald's wrapper in this trash can. Mine! Mine!"

You could argue that birds say what they mean and mean what they say. They're honest, straightforward, and upright creatures, but even the most anthropomorphic aviphile would have to allow that birds don't subscribe to metaphor. They may be poetry in motion to us, but they are not poets to themselves. Metaphor is an activity reserved for humans.

And because we are so reliant on symbols to express ourselves, we must always seek to know the names of things. Knowing the names of things is a shorthand way of knowing and understanding what these things do. Names also remind us of the stories we can tell and the meaning those stories have for us. When I tell someone I have just seen a Sharp-shinned Hawk at the Fill, as I did today, I mean that I have seen a bird that hunts other birds. It is a raptor that lurks in the foliage and comes bursting out to strike unsuspecting prey. It has short wings that allow it to maneuver adroitly. It looks a lot like its cousin, the Cooper's Hawk, but it is smaller and more delicate. It's not a popular bird when it shows up at the Fill. Other birds flee or attack it. Ducks explode into the sky to escape. Crows come from all over to dive-bomb the hawk and chase it away. Even the tiny hummingbird ventures forth to strike at the hawk. All this I know when I say, "I saw a Sharp-shinned Hawk today."

Perhaps our reliance on metaphor in language is what lies at the heart of our search for meaning in our lives. Humans need to understand how the world works—that's a control issue, a survival drive—but that is not all we need. We also need to understand *why* the world works that way. What does it all mean? Even more important, what do we mean to the rest of the world? Names do more than identify us; they tell the world why we matter, why everything we name matters.

Years ago, I visited Aransas National Wildlife Refuge in Texas. I was there to see the largest surviving flock of wild Whooping Cranes. In late fall, the cranes arrive at Aransas from their breeding grounds in the north and spend the winter in the marsh. The best way to see the cranes is to pay for a boat ride that takes you out on the water where the cranes forage. I'm too cheap for that, however, so the way I try to see cranes is to climb a tall wooden observation tower at the water's edge. From there, you can see for miles, and miles away is just where the cranes tend to be. You need a high-powered spotting scope to identify them because there are many large, white, wading birds at Aransas besides Whooping Cranes: Great Egrets, Snowy Egrets, Cattle Egrets, White Ibises, and the white versions of Reddish Egrets and Little Blue Herons. From a distance, they all look like tiny white specks.

One day, I was scanning the horizon for whoopers and coming up empty. After an hour of looking, I felt the tower shake as two people climbed up to join me. They were an older couple with a video cam. "Ooh, look," cried the woman, "there are the Whooping Cranes. Oh, take a picture of me standing in front of them," she said to her husband.

As he dutifully hauled out the video cam, I spoke up. "I have to tell you that what you're seeing out there are not the cranes. They are Great Egrets. Nice birds, but no cranes. I haven't seen any Whooping Cranes today. Just egrets."

They both gave me the stink-eye. Then in a loud voice, the woman said, "Dear, take a picture of me right here in front of the WHOOPING CRANES."

As the camera rolled, I shut up. What was I thinking? That couple would go home and show all their friends and relatives the video of their big trip to Texas. When they would come to the Aransas part, they would say, "Here's Betty, standing on the tower in front of the Whooping Cranes."

Everyone would crane forward and stare at the images—little white dots so small they could just as well be cotton balls floating in the marsh. Everyone would smile and say, "Wow, it must have been wonderful to see those Whooping Cranes." Betty would smile proudly, too. Everyone would be thrilled. No one would know that what Betty really saw were Great Egrets.

And maybe someday, if these people hear that the Whooping Cranes are in trouble and need money, they will remember the thrill they felt sharing those Whooping Cranes (not egrets!) with Betty. Remembering that, maybe they will open their wallets and give generously so that future generations might also see those magnificent birds, the WHOOPING CRANES.

May their name—and the names of all the wild's creatures—live forever.

5. Bushtit Magic

I used to read romance novels before I got married. In one story, the heroine had a crystal snow globe. One day she was feeling kind of lonely, so she picked up the snow globe and gazed into it. The scene inside was a one-horse sleigh filled with a laughing couple. Our heroine shook the globe, creating a flurry of "snow" around the couple. All of a sudden, she felt the universe tilt upside down on its axis. There was a moment of complete disorientation, and then poof! she was in the snow globe living the life of the sleigh riders.

You can see why I gave up reading romance novels—anyone who has been married as long as I have knows that the only magical "poofs!" you're ever going to have with your spouse are the ones you make for yourselves.

That's not to say that magic is absent from this all-too-real world of ours. As a matter of fact, I know exactly how that heroine felt when she was pulled into her snow globe. Today at the Fill, I was standing near the Wedding Rock, not thinking or feeling anything in particular. All of a sudden, a swirl of Bushtits came flying through. They must not have seen me until they were almost upon me, because some came so close their wings almost brushed my face. Instantly, I was enveloped in a flurry of feathers.

I don't know if you've ever had such an experience, but it is as enchanting as a fairy tale. You are literally caught up in the lives of these little birds, swept along with them in a tiny cyclone as they leap from one trembling leaf to another, then dive to the next bush to grab a bite of bug. Bushtits seem compelled to gossip as they go about their business. They keep up a constant chatter of high-pitched chips, reminiscent of a bevy of seventh-grade girls who haven't seen each other in, like, the past two hours at least. When the Bushtits enfold you in their flock, you feel that if you listened just a little bit harder, you would be able to understand every phrase.

I found myself twirling around and around, trying to keep up with them. I was smiling like a child. On my last twirl, I caught sight of a birder standing on the little stone footbridge at the entrance to the glade. He had frozen into immobility, as if turned to stone himself. Then we both exchanged a smile.

Among the many gifts birding has given me, the smiles I get from the pure beauty of birds must be the greatest. It is a gift for which I am very grateful, and it is the easiest of all gifts to share. Birding, for me, is closely tied to that sharing.

I remember one time my husband and I were out at the Brady Loop near Montesano in southwest Washington. It was early spring, although it might as well have been winter, it was so cold. We had stopped near the bridge to look over the riparian habitat for anything that moved. Birds were in there, but hidden. As we struggled to identify the birds and at the same time keep from turning into pillars of ice, we heard a car drive up. Who should tumble out but Ruth and Patrick Sullivan—Ruth the effervescent photographer, and her son Patrick, the brilliant young birder. After hugs and greetings, we all went back to the birds. My husband and I chatted with Ruth as we searched, but Patrick focused all his remarkable skills into the woods and pulled out a Yellow Warbler, the first of the season. With its golden feathers gleaming almost too brightly for the eyes, it was a little piece of sunshine that warmed us up. Who cares about bad weather when you're in the company of friends, doing what you love? You don't need words to explain how you feel. The eyes dance, the corners of your mouth turn up, and you are happy.

Part of that happiness, it seems to me, is an affirmation that everything is all right with the world. The sun continues to rise in the east and set in the west, just as it's supposed to do. The seasons turn, as they always have. The birds leave in the fall and come back in the spring, as they have done in the past and as they will continue to do in the future. The natural world has a pattern, a rhythm that is predictable and dependable. Things are okay. Life is good.

My belief in the general okayness of the world was shattered, however, when my family suffered an unexpected blow five years ago. Blows can be borne, I have discovered, if you have a little time to prepare for them. By contrast, a sudden blow that strikes at you from nowhere knocks you down so hard you don't know how you will ever be able to get up again.

My family survived by pulling together, as most people do at such times, but afterwards I fell into a worry spiral that would not let me go. The world was not okay anymore. I realized that the fairy tale doesn't always have a happy ending. Things don't necessarily turn out for the best. A window doesn't always open when a door is closed. Silver doesn't necessarily line the clouds. Bad things can happen to good people. The world is a chancy place.

People of faith evade the worry spiral because they believe that God is good. He has a plan for us, and it's a good plan. If something bad happens, we can be sure that there is a good reason for it. We may not understand God's reason; we may not agree with His plan. But at least we can trust that ultimately, He holds us in the palm of His hand, and everything will turn out all right, especially where it counts the most: in eternity.

People without faith in God still have faith in something, though I'm not sure what to call it. It has to do with believing that we know pretty much how the world works, and if we follow the rules of culture and nature, we'll be okay. Gravity will always be here, for example. You can count on it. If you drop a hammer, it's going to fall down, so you'd better get your foot out of the way.

But some of our belief in the general okayness of the world is more a child's trust that bad things simply won't happen, at least not to us. It's a faith that says when your teenage son takes the family car for a spin, he'll come back safe and sound. It's the trust that tells you when your husband kisses you goodbye in the morning and goes to work, he'll be home in time for dinner that night. He certainly won't get hit by a train, nor is he likely to run off with the nearest floozy. When I walk under the cottonwood trees that lean precariously over the path at East Point, I believe that I won't get killed by a falling limb, even though I see big limbs lying all over the ground, and I know they had to get there somehow. Just not on my head, just not right at that moment.

This belief is an illusion, and sometimes it cracks. In 2001, my writing students were working on an oral history book about World War II, and they interviewed a survivor of the Bataan Death March. Our interviewee wasn't sure at first that he wanted to talk about his experiences, but his wife convinced him to do it. She told him he had to tell young people his story so they would know not to ever let such a thing happen again. At the end of a harrowing interview, my students asked him what he made of it all. He said that even after more than 50 years, he had not been able to come up with an answer. "It's hard to develop one philosophy that works," he said, "where the bad get punished and the good survive. It doesn't quite work that way. The reason I'm alive? I was lucky."

After the kids went back to class, he told me that he had had a lot of trouble building his life again. He had seen too many haphazard acts of both kindness and cruelty. Good things happened to bad people *and* to good people; bad things happened to bad people *and* to good people. There rarely seemed to be a relationship, a cause and effect. It was mostly random, and "you can't build your life on random," he said.

Worry is one way to make the world seem less random because worry motivates you to plan ahead so you can avoid the blows that would otherwise fell you. As my Ukrainian-born daughter told me recently, "When you're living in a cave and a dark, big shape appears at the entrance, your first thought had better not be, 'Oh, that's only Grandma bringing us a tasty rabbit for dinner.' You need to be loaded for bear."

She's right. Worry is a great way to prepare for the worst if you happen to be a critter without fangs, claws, big ears, long legs, or wings—like us. On the other hand, worry is a good servant but a bad master. If the worry centers in our brains are turned on all the time, we can't function. We must have a haven where worry is locked out, a time when troubles can be set aside, a way to lay down our burden of fear and just be happy. For me, the Fill is that place, a refuge that restores and gladdens the heart.

When was the last time you smiled to express an overall sense of well-being? Smiled because all's right with the world, at least for now? Smiled just because the corners of your mouth couldn't help but turn up?

I can truthfully answer by saying, "I felt that way just an hour ago, when I was in the flock of Bushtits."

So if you feel down, don't waste another minute. Go out and find your own flock of Bushtits and twirl around with them for a while. If no Bushtits happen by, seek out a row of turtles and warm your back in the sun as they do. Or dance through a field of clover. You'll smile for the rest of the day. And as you smile, others will see you and smile back in happiness shared. It's magic.

6. Peace of Mind

As I write this, we are at war. It is a small war, as wars go. We have deployed roughly 140,000 troops in Iraq and some 20,000 in Afghanistan. We have 300 million people in the United States. That works out to be 0.05 percent of our population who are actively fighting. For the rest of us, the big concern is not the war. It is the falling economy. Our wallets.

The war has now lasted for seven years. In past wars of long duration, the entire nation made sacrifices. Everyone was affected. Not this time. This time, we are more focused on ourselves. The men and women who are far away fighting are also far away from our daily lives. Only those of us with loved ones in the war keep them in our hearts every waking moment and every sleepless night.

The thought enrages me. We should not be a country where so few make such large sacrifices, and the rest barely notice.

In the failing light of a winter evening, I took my rage to my favorite place on Earth, the Fill. I was hoping that the peace I usually find there in nature would suffuse my heart and dissolve away all the bad feelings.

I arrived as the fog was rising off the land. In the distance, the Husky marching band was practicing in the stadium. Their martial airs wafted past the fields like the rustle of a breeze. Across the lake, cars were rushing back and forth on the Floating Bridge, people hurrying home to warm houses and warmer suppers. All around me, I could smell the odor of the rank weeds that line the path to the Main Pond. I was alone with the wind and the birds.

I sat down on the north edge of the pond and tried to let the peace of the Green-winged Teals afloat on the still water fill my soul. But my soul was too crowded with darkness—no room for the peace I could see around me. I tried to attune myself to the ball of European Starlings bouncing over the cottonwoods in the distance. I listened quietly for the chipping note of a Golden-crowned Sparrow, down here from Alaska for the winter. To Golden-crowned Sparrows, the Fill is the balmy south, even when it snows here. I thought thoughts of calm. It was no use. The longer I sat, the more my rage bubbled up. Rage, and also grief—grief for the losses suffered by our troops and their families, including mine; grief for all the losses we inflict on each other and suffer for ourselves.

Where does war come from? Why anger, hatred, prejudice, greed? The ancient Greeks said these scourges on the soul of humanity entered the world because a foolishly curious Pandora opened the wrong box. Maybe so, but the Pandora's Box Theory of Original Sin didn't take the ancients very far down the road to understanding human nature. The blame game was just as unsatisfying 5,000 years ago as it is today.

Sociobiologists say that war is a part of human nature. We fight for more resources, they say, for more mates, for pride, for hatred of the other. But those are just excuses, another version of the blame game. For if I hate you, must I kill you? Can't I instead try to understand you, seek to find in you echoes of myself? If I have more than you do, must you kill me? Can't we find ways to share, or even better, can't we invent ways to increase resources for all of us?

I told myself, "You can't blame others for your own problems, nor can you just accept the ugliness of the world and let it go at that. No matter how many blows the world deals you, no matter how much others hurt you, you are still responsible for your own attitude and for your own actions. You may not control much in this world, but you can control that. Despair is not an option."

Myself wasn't listening. Instead, I was remembering a science fiction tale written years ago by Carol Severance. It's called "Whispering Cane." It's about a people, the Lelanin, who live in a land where they grow vast fields of sugarcane. When the Lelanin suffer a sorrow, they go to the fields, dig a hole, and scream their feelings into the land. When all the pain is deposited, they bury it. Their suffering nourishes the cane, which rustles with the voices of all the Lelanin who have lived and died in pain. As the story opens, the Lelanin are about to be overrun by an evil warlord. To save her people, the leader goes into the sugarcane fields, takes a knife, and slashes at the land, letting out the generations of suffering. The grief pours out and is so ghastly that all the enemies are overcome, just listening to the pain that others have felt.

Remembering that story, I imagined digging my own hole at the Main Pond and dumping all my bad feelings into it. I strained to give my grief and anger to the Fill, but nothing happened.

I sat there, watching the teals dabble gracefully on a glassy surface pocked now and then by misty raindrops falling from above. Finally, I packed up my stool and started back. There can be no connection to the serenity of nature when all your soul is stuffed with sorrow and anger.

My beloved Fill was failing me. Where can I turn for peace of mind if not here? I became so crushed with despair that I could not walk. I set my stool down at the south end of the pond and just stared dumbly at the scene. Then a slight motion along the shore caught my eye, and I beheld a Long-billed Dowitcher foraging at the water's edge.

Long-billed Dowitchers are shorebirds with preposterously long bills. They breed in the tundra of the Far North, and most of them spend the winter in the southern states and in Central America. However every year, a few elect to stay in Washington for the winter. When they overwinter in our state, they like to settle around freshwater ponds or brackish saltwater marshes. Every now and then, one pays a brief visit to the Fill, as this one was doing.

While I watched almost against my will, it strolled out of the water and began poking its Jimmy-Durantesque bill into the mud. A dowitcher's long bill looks hard and rigid, but in reality, it is loaded with sensitive nerves. The tips are flexible, so that when a dowitcher finds a tasty worm or crustacean deep in the mud, it can grab onto it and pull it out.

Eventually, the bird stopped eating and began preening, lifting its tail, opening its wings, stretching up its neck so its bill could reach its breast. When it was done, it tucked its bill into its back feathers and went to sleep. I quietly folded my stool and tiptoed back to the trail. In watching that goofy-looking but glorious bird go about its business, all my anger had leaked away, and I began to think clearly again for the first time in weeks.

It seems to me that people feel a need to control the environment and, through the environment, our lives. We seem to need the belief that by our actions, we can make ourselves safe. The religious among us pray to the Almighty, hoping He will intervene on our behalf. Those skeptical of religion live by the Boy Scout motto: be prepared. All of us hope we can stave off tragedy, disease, poverty, pain, and death. When we can't, we become afraid. The fear leads to anger.

I have learned that anger is not a good way to get through bad times. Anger can carry you for a while, enough to get you through an immediate crisis, perhaps. But it is no way to live. Anger shuts you away from love. It closes your eyes to beauty. It isolates you from the peace of mind that is nature's gift.

Why does nature grant peace of mind to us? Because nature is eternal. It is bigger than we are, bigger than the awful troubles that weigh us down.

The Fill is not a natural place, though nature is in it now. It was made by men cutting a canal and lowering Lake Washington, creating a new wetland, and then turning it into a landfill. When the dump was all filled with human garbage and dirt, men covered it over with a layer of clay and soil and gave it to nature.

Many of the plants that grow here were seeded by gardeners who can't seem to keep their hands off nature—the drive to modify the landscape and thus control it must be too strong. But many of the plants were brought by birds, and that is a key difference. Birds are wild and unpredictable. They do not obey any will of ours, but only their own.

This is a humbling thought, and a needful one—needful because it reminds us that we *cannot* control every living thing, nor every aspect of our own lives, no matter how much we try. Thus, we can let go of our guilt and our worries. We can let things be.

On some days when I come to the Fill, I see a Marsh Wren down at East Point, where the cattails grow thick. They provide the wren with both cover and a stage from which to sing. On many days, the wren sings with his big voice but hides from view. I can't see him no matter how long I wait or how skilled I am. I see him only if *he* decides to let me see him.

I don't know how much longer this particular Marsh Wren will make his home among the cattails at East Point. But I know that there will continue to be Marsh Wrens here long after I am gone, just as the Long-billed Dowitchers will continue to come here to feed in winter, preen their feathers, tuck their bills into their backs, and peacefully go to sleep. May that peace be upon us all.

7. A Rare Experience

Last week, my friend and fellow master-birder Evan Houston found a rare Short-eared Owl at the Fill. He said it was fluttering around in the fields at dusk, hunting for prey. Which brings up the whole issue of Dante's Inferno. In the mid-fourteenth century, Dante Alighieri, you may recall, wrote a massive tome of a poem about heaven and hell. He called his effort *The Divine Comedy,* the joke being on us.

Dante's poem was really a kind of map to the afterlife. In it, he charted three possible destinations for people who took the last, long journey: They could go to Paradise, the four-star hotel of the netherworld. They could go to Purgatory, a much less salubrious place. Or they could end up in Hell. Hell, said Dante, has nine circles, each more unpleasant than the last.

People whose travel destination is Hell or Purgatory don't have a choice about specifically where they go for their home-stay. They have a reservation waiting for them in a particular area. There's a spot for gluttons, another for hypocrites, and so on.

The reason I bring this up in the context of Evan's owl is that I can easily believe there is a special place in Dante's underworld reserved for people like me who chase rare birds. I know because I have often booked a room in my little corner of the underworld, though fortunately not on a permanent basis as yet. All serious birders have paid the same visit a time or two. We go there whenever we make a long and fruitless trip to see a rare bird that simply refuses to appear when or where we do.

The worst part of missing a rare bird occurs when we arrive at the distant destination, fling ourselves out of the car, throw on the binoculars/scope/hat/boots, and scurry up to the crowd of other birders, only to be told, "You should have been here five minutes ago." This is always said with a mixture of pity and smugness. It is then that we know we have just checked into Hell.

Medieval Christians such as Dante were not the only ones interested in describing the afterlife. As far as I can tell, pretty much every culture did this. In the ancient Greek version, dead souls are supposed to cross the River Styx, then spend their time drifting around incorporeally, awaiting the chance to drink from the River Lethe, forget their past lives, and return to the world as new souls. We learn about this version in many stories, among them the tale of how Orpheus traveled to Hell to fetch his beloved, Eurydice. Hell's bouncer, Charon, let Orpheus in without a cover because of Orpheus's outstanding ability to jam on the lyre. Not that that did Orpheus much good. As he was leading his beloved out of Hell, Eurydice couldn't resist the chance for one backward look, no doubt one of pity and smugness. That one glance condemned her to stay in Hell for eternity.

A terrific remake of this tale was written by novelist Richard Matheson and turned into a movie by Ronald Bass, entitled *What Dreams May Come,* starring Robin Williams as the Orpheus figure. In this movie, Heaven is a place where you can live in any kind of paradise you want. Each soul has merely to imagine a scene, and phut! it appears.

After watching this movie, I thought about what kind of a paradise I would imagine, if and when I arrive. It would include birding, of course, but a big part of birding for me is finding new, rare birds that I have never seen before. So naturally, being able to chase rarities would figure large in my version of Heaven.

Unfortunately, after imagining that, my mind boggles. Just exactly how would this scenario work? Let's say, for example, that I want to find a Bachman's Warbler. Bachman's is a little yellow wood-warbler with a black bib, gray nape, and white tail spots. It is thought to be extinct, but no one is sure. The last known sighting occurred in 1962 in the canebrakes of South Carolina. It would be great to find one, about as great as finding an Ivory-billed Woodpecker or an Eskimo Curlew, two species that are also thought to be extinct but maybe not.

So okay, here I am in Heaven, and I imagine walking through a canebrake, looking for a Bachman's Warbler. Do I see one? Well, since all I have to do is wish to see one, of course I do. But where's the fun in that, knowing that I can see the bird anytime I wish to? Okay, so do I *not* see the bird? Same difference—I just wish not to see it, and I don't. Do I make it hard to find? How hard? Five minutes hard? Five hours?

You see the problem. The element of chance is removed, and that removes all the challenge and all the fun. In order for a chase to really mean something, there has to be the real possibility of failure.

Back here on Earth, the possibility of failure is all too real. Because of Evan and his Short-eared Owl, I have gone to the Fill for the past several evenings, set up my camp stool near the Lone Pine Tree, and scanned the fields. As the sun slowly sets and I congeal in the cold, my scanning becomes more frantic. I stop noticing the way the sunset paints a wash of pink and gold across the horizon. I decline to appreciate the silhouettes of tree branches entwined in lacy outlines against the flaming sky. I am indifferent to the parade of American Wigeons streaming past me on their way to a duck convention on the Corporation Yard Pond. The Corporation Yard Pond is the ugliest and most polluted pond at the Fill. Why are the ducks drawn there? I have ceased to care.

"Come on, you stupid owl," I mutter, "show yourself."

Alas. Darkness descends, and at last I give up. I try to rise from my roost to go home, but I'm so frozen, I have to grab onto a tree limb to haul myself to my feet. Worse yet, I know I will be back on that stool again tomorrow night, and the next, and the next. I will shamelessly draw my husband there, too, so he can share in the experience. Washington is a community-property state, and he needs to own his half of the misery.

I can't say I'm happy to miss the owl so often and with such suffering. But not seeing birds is as much a part of our passion as

seeing them is. Birding, in fact, is a test of our skill, our knowledge, our imagination, but also our luck. We can be sure that we'll see a lot of birds if we practice our skills, learn everything we can about birds' habits, and try to figure out where a bird might be, given the season, weather, time of day, and habitat. But even then, we will need luck. The bird has to be there, and it has to be willing to appear. If it's casing some other joint or decides to sleep in, well, then we're going to miss it. Bad luck.

I think it's this last factor that produces such a spurt of joy when I see a great bird, rare or not. I feel happy, and not only because finding a great bird verifies my skill as a birder, so huzzah for me. I feel joy because the universe holds such beauty within it, and I have been given a chance to share it for a while. It is heavenly.

There is also a vision of Hell in the movie *What Dreams May Come*. Hell is where Robin Williams's fictional wife goes after she commits suicide. It is pictured as a ramshackle shack with not a single scrap of beauty in it. Not even color exists there. Everything is a kind of nondescript shade somewhere between gray and brown. When Williams arrives to bring his wife out of Hell, she refuses to go. The reason, Williams discovers, is that she believes she deserves to live in that eternally joyless shack. It is her own vision of Heaven, in a way.

I can't say what the afterlife holds for me. I do know, however, that there is plenty of heaven and hell right here on Earth. Like the characters in the movie, we often create it for ourselves. Hell on Earth is war, famine, poverty, ignorance, prejudice, hatred, fear. It is guilt, too, and cruelty. Self-doubt. It is all the things that hold us back from living in the light. We all have these demons within us, but we have divine angels that live in us, too, just as truly as do the darker forces. When we listen to their voices, we have the power to make ourselves and our world better.

Writer Tom Junod discovered this when he interviewed Fred Rogers (of Mr. Rogers fame) for a cover story he wrote for *Esquire* magazine in the November 1998 issue. He says in that story, "Once upon a time, a man named Fred Rogers decided that he wanted to live in heaven. Heaven is the place where good people go when they die, but this man, Fred Rogers, didn't want to go to heaven; he wanted to live in heaven, here, now, in this world, and so one day, when he was talking about all the people he had loved in this life, he looked at me and said, 'The connections we make in the course of a life—maybe that's what heaven is.'"

We make connections with each other and with nature in the here and now. They can be lasting connections or even brief ones—it doesn't really matter, so long as we recognize them when they come and remember them when they go. And so long as we realize that we have great power to make them for ourselves.

I make them for myself every time I smile at a child, or bake a pie for a friend, when I help my community by organizing our twentieth annual block party, or turn a nice phrase in an essay. Making a heaven on Earth is something anyone can do, in little ways or large, for the benefit of many or just for yourself. I do it whenever I go to the Fill, whether I see great birds or not, because there is always something there that I can connect with, some little bit of nature or friendship that always awaits me. When I find it, I feel a jolt go through me like lightning, electrifying my spirit. At such times, I have been known to dance for joy, split my face with a grin, and high-five whoever happens to be near. Sunshine fills my soul, even in the gray winter of Seattle, and I am in heaven.

It's that feeling I will seek tonight when I return to my perch under the Lone Pine Tree. The weather is supposed to be clear and cold, perfect for owls. You can come along, if you like. I know we'll find something good.

8. Beauty Is As . . .

A large flock of American Goldfinches were arguing on this winter day over who got to forage in the remnants of the Chicory, Queen Anne's Lace, and thistles left from the previous summer. The gardener for the Center for Urban Horticulture (CUH) has been busy with his tractor-mower since late August, cutting down all the plants and removing their seeds from one field after another. It's called weed control. The CUH folks are well aware that many of the plants that dominate the Fill are foreign invaders, indeed, noxious weeds. Mowing the fields before the weeds can re-seed is the best option to limit their spread.

The gardener would have finished mowing all the fields by September, but he was called away to work on other projects. So now in the wintertime, the birds can make the most of this last opportunity for easy pickings.

To my human eye, there seemed to be plenty of weeds to go around, but that is not what the goldfinches believed. They spent almost as much effort defending their chosen plant as they did eating the plant's seeds. At times, the defense got personal. In one case, I saw two goldfinches as they arrived at the same Chicory bush. They began to argue. The argument escalated from voices to blows, just as the birds themselves escalated, rising higher and higher into the sky, pecking, wing-beating, and trash-trilling each other. Finally, one goldfinch broke off and fled to a tree, but the other followed, and the fight resumed. The two mixed it up in the tree, becoming a finch ball of wings and beaks and feet, throwing blows too fast for the eye to see. Again, one fled, this time to a bush, but still the fight continued. Eventually, one goldfinch flew away, and the victor, figuratively dusting off its wings, looked around as if to say, "Well, that takes care of that. Now, where was I?"

At that point, it became clear the goldfinch had completely lost sight of where it was. The disputed territory, i.e., the original Chicory plant, had been taken over by a third party long ago. Unconcerned, the victor flew to an unoccupied Chicory and began to eat.

I had to ask myself what that bird had achieved. The territory it had claimed was lost to a third bird, and the Chicory it eventually commandeered had been vacant for some time. Why couldn't the two goldfinches have used diplomacy to achieve détente? Or why couldn't they have pulled an Alphonse and Gaston act when they had both arrived at the first Chicory? "After you, Alphonse." "No, my dear Gaston, after you." Or they both could have pulled up a chair and set to, each on a separate part of the plant. As my kindergarten teacher used to say, "Be nice and share." There was certainly enough to go around.

But sharing is not a value that birds put much stock in, nor is compassion or empathy. Maybe you need fur for that. Birds seem to have a colder, more reptilian approach to the gentler feelings. They do without. A Great Blue Heron chick, for example, will sometimes kill its siblings so as to maximize its own chance of survival. I've often seen birds viciously attack other birds for no apparent reason. The Mute Swan who used to live in the reeds near Webster Point would sometimes flap all the way across the bay to attack a harmless Canada Goose peacefully dabbling near the shore. Life is brutal if you're a bird.

I must admit I have seen occasional acts of kindness among birds, as when parents expend great efforts to feed their babies, but I don't think these actions represent true kindness as we humans understand it. Evolutionary biologist Richard Dawkins would say that the birds' care for their young is mere catering to the Selfish Gene, not kindness. In Dawkins's view, parent birds help their babies only in order to perpetuate their own DNA.

I remember observing this when a parent Virginia Rail raised a chick in the reeds near the curly willow tree. When the chick was old enough, the mom led him to the south end of the Main Pond, where she tried to teach him how to hunt for worms. She slid out cautiously from the bushes, one slow step at a time, ready to run back into hiding at the least sign of danger. When she reached the pond's shore, she began probing the mud for food. Instead of eating the worm she found, though, she gave a loud whistle, a call I had never heard before. Immediately, a little black fluff-ball scurried out of the bush, looked where his mom's bill was pointing, and snatched up the worm. Then he ran back into the bushes, while mom hunted for another morsel. Again came the whistle, the scurry, the helpful indication, the snarf.

It was entrancing to see the adult using her bill like a schoolteacher with a pointer, but I suppose a big part of the charm was its rarity. I've been trying to think of other acts of kindness I've witnessed among birds at the Fill, and I come up empty. To the contrary, I have many memories of "Nature, red in tooth and claw."

Which brings up this question: If birds are pure but cold beauty, how can they inspire such transcendent joy in my heart?

We humans find beauty in patterns and symmetry, probably because if we understand these aspects of nature, we can predict outcomes and prepare for them. This grants us control over our environment and helps us survive. I guess that's why many of us (especially architects!) find beauty in the repetitious glass windows and steel girders of modern-day skyscrapers. But although we find such patterns pleasing to the senses, even comforting in a mild way, transcendent beauty is a wholly different matter. For that, we need emotion, hence relationship. And this leads to love.

When two people find each other attractive, they sometimes fall in love. They tell each other, "You are beautiful," but what they really mean is, "You are beautiful in my eyes."

If they are lucky, they get married and live a long and happy life together. In their old age, they can still look at each other and say, "You are beautiful," when in fact, objectively they are jowly, saggy, and wrinkly. Do their eyes deceive? No, said my mother-in-law at her 40th wedding anniversary. I asked her why she had never left her somewhat unsatisfactory husband, and she said, "You don't simply walk away from 40 years of a shared life."

Now that I have been married for more than half that time, I can see her point. My husband and I have lived through many experiences, good and bad. We have leaned on each other for strength in time of need, and we have laughed together at all times, even in the midst of tears. But when I look at him, I don't see our memories floating about him like cartoon bubbles. Memory plays almost no part in the way I see him. I do remember that I fell in love with him at first sight. I thought he was a knight in shining armor. He had curly, chestnut hair, a killing smile, strong arms, laugh lines around his eyes. He was handsome, and yes, I told him so.

Is he still handsome? That's hard to answer. When I look at him now, I do notice what he looks like—whether his hair is tousled or combed, whether he has chosen to wear a bright bow tie or a somber one. I see these things, but only superficially, because I am drawn to look deeply past the outward envelope. It's as though the outward appearance is nothing more than a suit of clothes that he can change from day to day. But changing his outfit changes nothing of the man himself. It does not change who he *is*, his spirit, the force of life itself that he embodies, unique unto himself. A religious person would call it his soul. That is what I see when I see him now, and that will always be beautiful to me.

Star Trek writer Michael Michaelian understood this when he wrote the episode, "Too Short a Season." The story involves Admiral Mark Jameson, an old diplomat who is called upon to negotiate the release of hostages on a planet he had inadvertently plunged into civil war 40 years ago. Jameson knows this assignment will take every ounce of his energy, and so he gulps down an alien drug designed to restore his youth. The drug works, and Jameson becomes young again, but the drug's ultimate effects are fatal. As he lies dying in his 80-year-old wife's arms, he looks up at her and says, "Annie of the golden hair."

She smiles tenderly. "Flatterer, it's gray now."

With his last breath, he says, "I see only the gold."

So it is with all the things and people we love. We see past the outward envelope and deep into the ideal. Beauty gives us a lens to focus our eyes so that we can see the *essence* of what and whom we love. My husband was beautiful to me when I first met him, and he is more beautiful to me now. He will always be so.

That is why I can notice that the Fill does have rotting tires sticking up here and there, birds do live stark emotional lives that usually end badly, the world contains much ugliness. Yet none of these things matter when it comes to my deepest understanding of beauty, just as a few wrinkles and gray hairs do not matter at all. My spirit soars on wings of joy when I look at the people and things I love, and I love the Fill. To me, the Fill is a lens for all of nature, for our planet, and for the boundless richness of life. It is awful, in the divine sense, and beautiful beyond words.

I see only the gold.

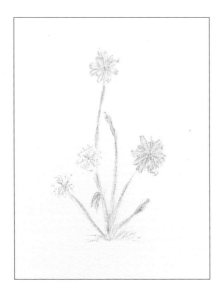

Part II
Spring

9. Comings and Goings

When my mother was a girl, she used to walk down to the train station in the center of South Bend, Indiana, find a seat on one of the oak benches with the carved seat backs, and watch the people come and go. She loved to imagine the stories they could tell, the places they had been, the destinations still to come.

Some of the people were clearly arriving. Their families would stand by the gate with hopeful expressions, scanning all the faces as strangers streamed by. My mother could always tell when such families were waiting to be reunited with long-lost loved ones because everyone would be dressed up in Sunday best, including little boys in short coats and little girls looking like Easter. The little girls always held flowers.

My mother found it just as easy to tell the people who were departing. They were the ones who left their tears behind.

Back in those days, travel to distant places was rare. Most people tended to stay put, although there were always a few who had the yen or the need to travel. Fiddle-foot, they were called sometimes, or immigrants, or even DPs—displaced persons from the wars.

I was reminded of my mother's stories yesterday at the Fill as I sat on the shores of the Main Pond. A group of Ring-necked Ducks paddled nervously at the north end, eyeing me with suspicion. They were newcomers. None had been here the day before, and none would stay till the next day either. They were on their way north and east to breed, anxious to leave, waiting for the night, when nature's train whistle would sound in their minds and they would rise up and be gone.

On the lake, armadas of Common Mergansers hunted for fish. They were serious about their work because they had to build up their stores of fat, packing their bags, as it were, for their trip to the breeding grounds. They looked like submarines as they powered along the surface, leaving a little wake behind. Every few feet, they scanned for fish, dipping their heads until their eyes were underwater like an upside-down periscope.

The mergansers meet here every year in the spring. My mother would have said they were like a tour group, loosely gathered in ones and twos, getting acquainted before taking off on their trip to Alaska. A big adventure. Birders call this "staging." For days, the mergansers come from all parts south to this place. Once here, they linger. The fish are abundant, and except for the occasional eagle, the waters are safe. Each year, the mergansers look like they'll be here for months, but looks can deceive. One night, they'll decide it's time, and they'll be gone, along with the other ducks that come here in the fall, stay for the winter, but breed in faraway places: the Buffleheads, Canvasbacks, Green-winged Teals, scaups, and Northern Pintails. All of them come here for just a while, but all of them leave, too, as they have done for 10,000 years.

I'm always a little wistful to see them go, as my mother must have been, sitting in the train station, watching other people having adventures. I wish I could go with the birds and have adventures, too, but I have duties here, people to take care of, a job to do, a yard to mow. For now, I am a fixed point in time and space and must wait for the birds to come to me.

Luckily, I don't have long to wait. It is spring, after all, and our summer residents from the south have begun to arrive, even as the last of our winter birds disappear. Each new day in spring brings someone new to welcome home again.

Today, April 23, the Vaux's Swifts showed up for the first time this year. They're punctual. I've checked my notes from past years: April 21, April 22, April 24. I was getting a bit worried about them because the weather this year has been so cold. It snowed on April 20, and for several days prior, setting one record after another.

I was glad to be at the Fill this day to greet the swifts and the other spring arrivals, despite the sleet, hail, snow, rain, and freezing winds. It wasn't easy. The calendar fooled me into thinking it was spring, so I went out completely underdressed, wearing only shirtsleeves, lightweight pants, and a fleece vest.

The Finns say there is no such thing as bad weather, only inadequate clothing. Cold comfort for me, as I sat on my camp stool and slowly solidified. I thought about something raptor expert Bud Anderson had told me during a class about the raptors of the Skagit. He asked us to think about what it would be like to be a bird. "You can't go home to a heated house when you get cold," he said. "You can't come in out of the rain. You have to eat something every day or two or you die, but you can't just go into the kitchen and open a can of something or order out. You have to hunt for prey and kill it, and then you have to keep others from stealing it." We students began to realize that if we were birds, we'd all be dead.

I often think about Bud's empathy exercise, especially when I'm at the Fill. Central Puget Sound used to be a busy way station for millions of birds flying north to breed, and for those same birds and their offspring flying south for the winter. Today, there is not a single patch of natural saltwater mudflats left in King County. The old-growth forests are long gone. The riparian habitat that lined our rivers has largely been replaced by bike paths, docks, parking lots, and pavement.

The Fill has little bits and pieces to offer the birds. There are a few freshwater mudflats, but they occur only in a narrow strip around the Main Pond year-round and in even smaller patches around the temporary ponds in the spring. There is a little prairie habitat in fields to the north and south of Wahkiakum Lane, but it is always threatened by encroaching blackberry and willow. A few stands of tall cottonwoods and alder take the place of old-growth, but the groves are small and scattered, allowing in a multitude of predators and parasitic cowbirds. Riparian habitat flourishes, but only in small quantities around two sloughs, a pond, and two tiny swamps. True forest is nonexistent.

Into this miniature area of about 75 acres, the birds must all fit themselves. They share the place with thousands of humans who come here for a variety of reasons. In 1994, the University of Washington reported the results of a small survey conducted to help determine how best the Fill might be used. The survey (published in *Management Plan for the Union Bay Shoreline and Natural Areas owned by the University of Washington*) discovered that many UW people use the Fill for class field trips, research, student theses and projects, continuing education programs, and nature study. The College of Engineering brings students to the Fill to teach them how to use surveying instruments. The ROTC trains here. The School of Art has a small ceramic and metal arts shop on the site, and Facilities has yards here for maintenance equipment. The intercollegiate sports folks schedule softball games, Ultimate Frisbee, and rugby matches in the fields just to the north, and this year, the Washington Boomerang Club hosted the World Boomerang Championships there.

The general public uses the Fill in massive numbers as well, for all manner of activities—jogging, strolling, dog-walking, bird-watching, picnicking, meditation. People come here to grab a little bit of the outdoors, to fly kites and model airplanes, to fish, to practice music, and to photograph and paint nature. Many use the main trail as a commuter's route to get to and from campus or Husky Stadium. The Center for Urban Horticulture rents space for outdoor weddings and holds massive plant sales for the general public. Their buildings house classrooms, meeting rooms, offices, and a first-class horticulture library, open to all. A Youth Garden introduces young people to the challenges and joys of gardening. The UW Waterfront Activities Center nearby rents canoes and rowboats so that people can boat here.

The Fill successfully accommodates all these users—including more than 240 species of birds who live or pass through here—but only as long as everyone respects one another and as long as everything stays in balance. Respect and balance are not really such a tall order, if we value the place enough to make the effort. Value is the real key.

Such was not the case with the South Bend train station where my mother used to sit. The train station is empty now. No trains stop there anymore, no people bustle in and out. No one has found a new use for the handsome old building. It sits there quietly, unvalued, a reminder of how things used to be.

How much value should we place on the Fill?

It is no exaggeration to say that the Montlake Fill is a unique way station and home for wildlife in an urban area. "Unique" in the common usage of our language often means unusual or rare, but the actual definition of the word is: "one and only." There is only one Montlake Fill in all of Seattle, in all of Washington State, in all the world. It is incalculably valuable, crucially useful.

The birds know this—it is why so many depend on it. I hope we humans know it, too.

10. A Little Story

Spring days dawn early in the high latitudes of the Fill, but if you can drag yourself out of bed by 5:00 a.m. and get down there at sunrise, you will find a private paradise. On a clear morning, the sun reaches out rosy fingers to caress the treetops with the first warmth of the day. The air slides over your skin like a silken sheet, making you shiver with more than the chill of the fog that lies serenely in the dales. American Robins fly from tree to tree, their molten copper breasts glowing so brightly they might as well be wearing "Eat me" beacons for passing raptors. But the passing raptors pass on, looking for other prey.

I've sometimes wondered if the reason why robins are so brazen about their presence is because they taste bad. Maybe that's why they don't care who sees them. Usually when they fly to a new perch, they pick the topmost branch. They announce their arrival with a loud chirp and then look around, as if daring anyone to come after them. If no enemy appears, robins often throw back their heads, open their beaks, and pour forth their music, nearly closing their eyes in the ecstasy of their own brassiness. Not your shy wallflower, by anyone's definition.

Contrast this to their cousins, the Hermit Thrushes, who skulk in the deepest shadows, their sober brown backs, russet tails, and spotted breasts blending into the foliage. Hermit Thrushes seldom come out into the open to sing for an audience, although their song is nothing to be ashamed of. On the contrary, some say the echoing, fluted measures of the Hermit Thrush's song are the most beautiful music in the woods. Yet seeing the performer is nigh impossible.

I know because I have often tried. In the spring when I hear a Hermit Thrush's song float out from the cottonwood grove that arches like a cathedral over the Loop Trail near East Point, I hurry over there as fast as any paparazzo on the celebrity prowl. When I arrive, panting, at the nave, I look around frantically for the singer. Usually in vain. The celestial voice has stopped, the singer has retreated deeper into the shadow, and I am left with only the memory of the music, slipping away into the wine air.

Not to worry, though. Other singers take the thrush's place: the robins, of course, but also the wood-warblers, who are arriving from the south each day and who linger here awhile to fuel up before they sing their way north; the Bewick's Wrens, who are revving up their solos so they can compete for females; and the House Finches and American Goldfinches, who are hard at work on their complex harmonies. It is all wondrously beautiful.

I remember one spring day so glorious with song that I looked around for someone to share it with. The beauty was just too big for one person. Luckily, I saw a stranger hiking along the Loop Trail, and I went forward eagerly to meet her. It didn't matter that I had never seen her before in my life—she wore the birder's uniform: good walking shoes, long pants to protect against brambles and bug bites, one of the "Vests of a Dozen Pockets" that you see in outdoor catalogs (though nobody I know ever fills more than two pockets with anything), a ratty hat, and expensive optics. I figured no birder is truly a stranger, and I was bursting with the joy of the day.

"Isn't this the most beautiful place on Earth?" I gushed. "I just heard a Hermit Thrush singing, and a bunch of Savannah Sparrows are out there in the field keeping time, and the American Wigeons are applauding, and... " My voice trailed off. The stranger was eyeing me like a French waiter who has just been informed there's a beetle in the bouillabaisse.

"Well, yes, a Hermit Thrush is nice," she conceded, "but don't you realize how polluted this place is? You make it sound beautiful, but really it's sick. The birds aren't healthy, you know." Then she strode on out of sight.

I don't know about you, but if the Devil ever pops up out of Hell on one of my walks, as soon as the sulfurous fumes have cleared and he offers me a deal, I would be tempted to ask for the ability to make a quick rejoinder. I can't tell you how many times in my life I've been caught flat-footed by a quick-witted critic whose barb pierces my brain, paralyzing me like a jellyfish victim. By the time I've thought of a good reply, days have passed, sometimes years.

Meanwhile, in the interval between the jab and my Johnny-come-lately counterpunch, I replay the person's remarks over and over. Could they be true?

Face it: the Fill *is* polluted. It is a former garbage dump, after all. Rotting tires still work their way to the surface now and then. The methane burners that used to roar with flame night and day no longer belch, but you can see methane bubbles burbling in the ponds whenever a low-pressure front moves in. The little potholes in the prairie glisten with rainbows, but they're not the kind of rainbows Dorothy sings about. They come from the oil that floats on the puddles' surfaces.

The birds don't seem to mind, though. To my eye, they thrive. Many species breed here or stop for a quick meal during migration. Are they all getting sick from the miasma that rises invisibly from below? Maybe I ought to stop eating the blackberries that ripen in the fall—I don't want to glow in the dark. Cry, my beloved Fill.

But no matter how loudly that horrible woman's voice keeps echoing in my brain, I cannot cry. The Fill simply does not inspire tears in me. I don't go there to get dragged down. I go there to be lifted up.

Nevertheless, as I have thought about that woman's words over the years (still vainly trying to come up with a retort!), I have come to see a profound truth in what she said. When she and I met on the path, we stood under the same trees. We breathed the same air, heard the same sounds. The grass waved in the breeze for her as much as it did for me. Tree Swallows swooped over her head and mine, looking down on both the works of man and nature as they searched the sky for food.

She and I gazed upon the exact same facts, but the way we interpreted those facts was wildly different. Whenever I look at the Fill, I see a place that used to be a landfill but is now a nature reserve. I see an example of people fixing up the world. I see wild nature in the heart of a city. I see birds so glorious I sometimes feel my spirit leave this earth and fly off into the blue, soaring with wings almost as real to me as any possessed by a hawk or a swift. When she looked at the Fill, she saw the ugliness that humans excrete by the Dumpster-load. She saw the poison. I saw the paradise.

Who was right? We both were.

Perhaps the most profound truth about human existence is that we are story-tellers and story-listeners. The cold, dry facts of the merely physical are not enough for us. We are driven to find meaning in them. We must know the answers: Why am I here? What is my purpose? What does it mean?

Stories give us the answers.

Birds don't have that, nor do they need it. In their world, the laws of nature are stark: When the falcon comes for them, they're either strong enough to escape or they're toast. When the weather turns cold, they either find enough food or they die. The strong survive. The weak perish. The mother Gadwall starts with eleven chicks, and each day she loses one—to the carp, to the bullfrog, to the raccoon or the heron. She has no teeth or claws to protect them. She must breed a lot because she loses a lot.

The laws of nature govern us humans as much as they govern all physical things in the universe, but they do not *control* us. Why? Because we bring into the world the ability to interpret events any way we want. We create meaning.

Let's say, for example, that you are driving to work and someone cuts you off. In Seattle, this is a daily occurrence that often produces road rage, as you fume about the inconsiderate oaf who ought to be punished; at least he should get a ticket, but where are the cops when you need them? As you contemplate the injustice of it all, your anger grows exponentially. Boy, could you give the universe a piece of your mind.

Scientists tell us that the desire for payback is deeply embedded in our nature. Tit for tat, they call it. Tit for tat tells you that when a lout cuts you off in traffic, your natural response is to try to cut him off in return. If you can't do that, then your desire for tat might lead to a wish to bring forth your bazooka and *blammo!* Problem solved.

Fair enough. But notice that in this scenario, I have told a whole story with just one word: lout. A lout is someone who does not deserve kindness. Tit for tat is the only thing a lout can understand. In fact, you owe it to the world to get back at that lout and teach him a lesson—maybe if you do, the lout will behave less loutishly next time, and you will be a hero for making the world a better place.

But what if I told a different story? What if I said that the guy who cut you off was a father whose child had been severely injured, and he was rushing her to the hospital in a desperate attempt to save her life? Then shouldn't your own humanity dictate that you slow down immediately and let him in?

Or what if I said that the driver was late for the last flight to Dubuque, where her frail, elderly parents were celebrating their 50th wedding anniversary, and this was her best chance to reconcile with her family after years of silence? Just think how much good you could do by making it possible for that woman to catch her flight.

The point is, any of these three stories could be true, and there is absolutely no way for us to learn which one is right. Therefore, why not tell ourselves a story that helps us feel and act better?

As a free-lance writer, I often submit stories to magazine editors, hoping they'll be accepted for publication. Occasionally, I get back the thin letter of rejection instead of the fat envelope of the contract. When this happens, I *could* tell myself the story of how I thought I was a good writer, but obviously I am not because a reputable editor thinks my stuff stinks. Or I could tell myself the story of how my submission unfortunately arrived on the desk of a reader who just didn't like my style, and if I try to find a different reader next time, I will likely succeed. Anne Frank's *The Diary of a Young Girl* was turned down fifteen times, with one reader calling it "a dreary record of typical family bickering." It currently has 30 million copies in print. George Orwell's *Animal Farm* was rejected because, as one of the editorial readers said, "It is impossible to sell animal stories in the USA."

When I get the dreaded rejection letter in the mail, it's obvious how I should interpret the facts. I won't tell myself the "you're a bad writer" story because that will do nothing to help me lift up my heart and try again. I like the "they're a bad editor" story much, much better. For if we are to move forward and achieve our goals, then we need to see ourselves as capable of such achievement. If instead we tell ourselves a hopeless story that gives us a good excuse to sit on our hind ends and do nothing, then nothing will get done.

Notice that I'm not saying we should try to sugarcoat the truth. I am saying that the deepest truths about ourselves are not set in

cement by the way that others see us, or even by the way we see ourselves. We can change, but we must try. The best way to try is to tell ourselves a story that gets us moving again.

And not every story has to be a happy-face one. In 1991, I interviewed Alice Houston, the assistant superintendent of Seattle Public Schools. Houston was an innovative educator who, among many achievements, founded a successful program that gave dropouts a second chance. Houston told me she had been born in the South during the height of Jim Crow laws. All her life, she had heard bad messages about how she would never achieve anything because she was black. The story she told herself about these experiences boiled down to three words: "I'll show them." And she did.

Life deals us many blows. No matter how much we plan or how careful we are, we cannot avoid them all. Stuff happens. But what we make of the things that happen is truly up to us and to the meaning we ourselves inject into our own lives.

Author Robert Penn Warren knew this. In his book *All the King's Men*, his lead character, a corrupt, populist Louisiana politician, explains how to deal with political dirt—and with life in general:

"'Dirt's a funny thing,' the Boss said. 'Come to think of it, there ain't a thing but dirt on this green God's globe except what's under water, and that's dirt too. It's dirt makes the grass grow. A diamond ain't a thing in the world but a piece of dirt that got awful hot. And God-a-Mighty picked up a handful of dirt and blew on it and made you and me and George Washington and mankind blessed in faculty and apprehension. It all depends on what you do with dirt.'"

Life is what you make of it. Life is the story you tell.

11. Eagles in Spring

A pair of Bald Eagles is making a brand-new nest near the northeast corner of the Fill. I've been privileged to watch how they do it, step by step. They start by fetching extremely large branches with their feet. This past winter brought many storms that created windfalls in the nearby woods, so the eagles have plenty of material. After picking up a good-sized branch, they flap over to their chosen tree crotch, aim, and let go. Their aim is none too accurate, so it's wise not to stand very near during this part of the process—you could get hit by a falling branch.

With enough bombing runs, the eagles eventually begin to create a mound of randomly stacked branches lodged helter-skelter in a tree crotch. I suppose it gets easier to hit the target as the target gets bigger. This particular pair began hitting two targets in the same tree, so now there is a big ramshackle nest in one crotch and a much smaller nest in another crotch below—kind of a mother-in-law apartment, you might say.

I suspect the female eagle may have already laid an egg or two because there's usually someone crouched low in the nest. I can't tell if it's the dad or the mom. Eagle genders look alike to the nonavian eye. The nest appears to be extremely uncomfortable. What keeps the birds from getting poked by their sticks? Eagles do line their nests with soft grasses and such, but they never seem to bring as much padding as you'd think they would need. Speaking for myself, I can't rest easily at night if even a single crumb from my husband's pesky habit of eating toast in bed lands on my side, which it frequently does. I guess I'd make a very bad eagle.

At first glance, the tree chosen by these eagles is problematic. It's right next to a street, and the neighbors have begun to gawk. One man was out there yesterday taking pictures. Normally, eagles like their privacy, but this pair regally ignores their many fans. The eagle who happens to be sitting on the nest gazes out over the heads of the people below, never even looking down. The other one often perches on a nearby branch and is equally oblivious to the hoi polloi.

Perhaps if one lives high above the common herd, one inevitably gets elevated ideas about oneself. With the sun shining on their gleaming white heads, and the blue sky for a backdrop, these two eagles look every inch the National Bird. Thomas Jefferson must have seen just such a pair in his day, which is probably why he was such a partisan for making the Bald Eagle our national symbol. Indeed, the Bald Eagle appears on the Great Seal of the United States carrying olive branches in one foot and arrows in another, both clutched against the day when they can be dropped, somewhat randomly no doubt.

Benjamin Franklin, a far more practical man, wanted to make the turkey our national bird. He said the eagle was "a bird of bad moral character," a thief and a coward.

I wouldn't go so far as to agree with Franklin about the cowardice charge, but it is certainly true that Bald Eagles are not above a little thievery, if they think they can get away with it. Today, for example, I heard a Peregrine Falcon "kekking" her complaints as she came winging in from Shoveler's Pond, empty-clawed. She perched in one of the alder trees over my head and kept kekking. After venting her displeasure for another few minutes, she flounced off, still kekking. I looked around, trying to find the source of her rage, and then I saw one of the eagles bringing a big, fat coot to the nest. Ah, the boodle.

It was just such actions as this that gave Franklin the pip about Bald Eagles. He wanted a more noble, more honest bird to symbolize our country. Failing that, he said, the turkey—while a little vain and silly perhaps—was at least edible. Sometimes I wonder how much our history would have changed if we had adopted Franklin's prosaic suggestion.

I suppose our present-day eagles selected this very public site because their nest tree is near Union Bay, which is full of fish, coots, and ducks, the eagles' favorite foods. Hunting, for the eagles, must be almost as easy as going to the deli is for us. Whenever they get hungry, they fly over to the bay and take a look at what the smorgasbord is offering today. If fish is on the menu, one eagle simply folds its wings, plummets down, and grabs. If the fish is small, the eagle performs what airline pilots call a touch-and-go: down briefly for the touch, and then up again for the go, this time with fish in claw. If the fish is big, there is a mighty splash, and the eagle rests briefly on the water, working up the energy to lift off again with its heavy burden.

One day a few weeks ago, I saw either Ma or Pa Eagle catch a fish so huge, no eagle could have hefted it. Rather than let go of its catch, however, the eagle took a firm grip and began to flap its way over to a floating log, skating along the surface like a surfer who had lost his wave. I suspect that the eagle had been planning on taking its fish back to the nest to feed the other parent, who was brooding the eggs and guarding them against predatory crows. When this proved impossible, the eagle made the best of the situation and ate the fish in situ. Apparently, eagles have a practical side that even Benjamin Franklin could have admired.

Sometimes American Coot is the specialty du jour. When this happens, the eagles like to hunt in tandem if possible. One eagle begins by herding a flock of coots together out on the lake. Then each eagle makes a flying pass at the flock, diving down low but not trying to snatch anything. The coots are absolutely terrified, naturally. After the eagles go by, they rise up on the water and churn their feet as they try to escape. You can hear the splashing from the shoreline a hundred yards away. As soon as the eagles begin to make another pass, the coots stop running and huddle down in a big bolus. If coots had fingers, no doubt they would be crossed, each little coot hoping that its neighbor will be chosen.

Meanwhile, the eagles hope that one coot will be too weak or too dumb to keep up with the flock. If a coot does become separated from its fellows, the eagles fly back and forth above the hapless bird, making it dive underwater each time. Eventually, the coot wears out and the eagles have their dinner.

Ma and Pa Eagle have been hunting the coots so relentlessly all winter that the coots seldom swim far from shore anymore. They hunker down near the cattails and twitch a lot.

The American Wigeons, who, like the coots, also used to swim far out on the lake ante-eaglum, have now elected to huddle on the Main Pond. They know that eagles love to eat the occasional duck, if they can catch one. For some reason, the ducks eschew hiding among the cattails with the coots. They seem to think they are safe as long as they stick together on the pond. Sometimes there are as many as a thousand clustered together there. When a dog comes by, the ducks are faced with a dilemma: to flee from the dog and risk the eagles, or to stay and hope the dog's leash is strong. Usually, the wigeons call excitedly to each other until the cacophony sounds like a merry-go-round gone wild, but they don't actually do anything. By the time the group comes to consensus (do we go or do we stay?), the canine crisis has walked on down the trail. Whew.

My husband and I are eagerly looking forward to the day the eagles' eggs hatch. It will be fun to watch someone else take care of newborns. I still shudder when I remember the countless sleepless nights we endured, as John and I walked around and around until our screaming baby finally went to sleep. If the light catches it right, you can still see a faintly worn path in the dining room carpet, a result of the track we tramped into the nap as we trudged the room, fussy baby strapped to the chest. Now our kids are grown men and women, out there building their own nests and hunting down their own dinners. It's hard to believe how fast the years have flown.

12. Chores Undone

I am neither a house-proud nor a yard-proud person. I don't need to have the most imposing home, nor the most artistic landscape. But I do have one little ambition, one little standard, however low. I yearn not to have the worst yard on the block. So long as even one other person has more of a junkyard look than I do, I'm happy. Second-worst is fine by me. I am content with my dandelions, my clumpy grass tussocks, the moss crowding out the blue-stem in ever-widening circles. I can tolerate even the one patch of dirt upon which nothing ever grows. I have never sought to learn why this one spot stays so stubbornly bald. As my husband has often counseled, "Don't ask questions to which you do not want to know the answers."

But today was going to be different. Today I had scheduled the entire morning for yard work. I was determined to toil until my yard made it into the top ten, at least. I had my weeding stool set to go by the front door, my gardening gloves, my sun hat. The weather was so perfect it could only be produced by a Seattle April: blue sky, puffy white clouds, not too hot, no mosquitoes. Time to get cracking.

Alas, instead of rolling up my sleeves and getting to work, I went to the Fill. I intended only a short walk, just a quick look at the Main Pond to see if any new shorebirds had flown in during the night. April is the month when a vast river of migrating birds flows from the south through the Puget Sound Trough to the breeding grounds in the far north. Washington State hosts more than three dozen different species of shorebird, and you can see a lot of them at the Fill in the spring.

I always feel that if I skip a day birding in April, I might miss seeing the only Greater Yellowlegs of the season, or possibly my best view of a Long-billed Dowitcher in breeding plumage. Greater Yellowlegs are sandpipers with long, bright-yellow legs. They deck themselves out in black and white polka dots in the spring, an avifaunal Harlequin onstage with the Jimmy Durantes of the bird world, the dowitchers. Dowitchers have ridiculously long beaks that they use to probe in the mud for worms and crustaceans. It's easy to picture them sticking a cigar in their bills and exiting stage left with a "Hot-cha-cha-cha."

Unfortunately, as Socrates said, "Know thyself," so I should have known better than to go to the Fill at all. Once there, I couldn't bring myself to leave. I tried three times to return to the chores awaiting me at home, and each time, some new bird drew me back. The first time, I was actually in my car with the motor running, but then I heard a Killdeer calling from the Dime Lot. Naturally, I had to go there to find the Killdeer. I also wanted to check on the Warbler Tree.

Birds have a funny habit of patronizing one bush or tree and ignoring others that look exactly the same to our eyes. The Warbler Tree is a case in point. It's a willow on the banks of University Slough, down where the Old Wooden Bridge used to be. Songbirds have favored this tree for decades. You can find it by looking for the concrete pylons that used to support the bridge but now support only the occasional perching songbird. In the mornings, you should stand on the east side of the tree in the Dime Lot so you get the full benefit of the rising sun at your back. In the afternoons, you can cross the New Wooden Bridge at the north of the lot and walk down a service road to get the western sun at your back. Be patient and keep looking through the leaves just curling out of their winter sheaths. Here be warblers.

Here also on this day was a Greater White-fronted Goose floating in the slough. It's a guy who has been hanging around the Fill all winter, in company with the resident Canada Goose flock. This bird will be leaving soon for the far north. In fact, the goose was already late, although he frankly didn't look prepared to head out any time soon. However, the call of migration is strong, and I knew that on this night or perhaps the next, our winter visitor would start churning his feet, flapping his wings, and voicing his call. Using the slough as a runway, he would take off and wing his way north.

All the winter residents who have used the Fill as a refuge for the past several months will leave soon, too—most have already gone. But I figured there was still a chance to see a few hangers-on. It would be nice to say good-bye and wish them well, so off I went to the Main Pond. There, sure enough, was a little flock of four American Pipits feeding at the north end.

American Pipits always make me think of robins that have seen a ghost and lost all their color. Instead of the rich red of the robin's breast, pipits' fronts are a pale ecru with a few darker stripes here and there. Pipits show up at the Fill in the winter to forage for bugs in the grass or for worms in the mud, but they breed in Alaska. These four would soon leap into the sky to circle the fields one last time. They would give the musical "pip-eet" call of their own name and then disappear into the north, leaving me behind, unable to fly, unable to sing pip-eet, unable to follow. Ah, me.

No need for regrets, though, because an early summer resident was also present on the Main Pond. Asleep on the far shore was a Blue-winged Teal with his bill tucked into his back. The slash of white crescent on his face was just visible above the brownish feathers on his back, creating a dramatic contrast. Blue-winged Teals are even more dramatic when they spread their wings and you can see the powder-blue that gives them their name. I set down my camp stool to wait for the duck to awake and show me his wings. When at last he did, I smiled in perfect contentment and stood, ready to go home to take up my responsibilities again.

But then a group of birders clustered around a spotting scope to the west drew me over there. They were looking at a pair of Cinnamon Teals, a male and a female. With the sun shining on the rich mahogany of the male's flanks, the bird was a glorious symphony of warm tones: red eyes, honey tertials, glowing embers on the sides. Then this gorgeous creature casually flipped out a webbed foot and scratched his head, ruffling the perfection of those lovely feathers. It was rather like a graceful Siamese cat who, completely conscious of its own beauty, poses for the adoring masses but then heaves up a hairball. And so back to reality.

I was trudging my way to the car and my yard work when a group of birders at Shoveler's Pond told me they had just seen a Yellow-headed Blackbird foraging east of the Main Pond. Yellow-headed Blackbirds are common in Eastern Washington but rare here. Why fight it? Back I went, to see a gorgeous male with lemon-yellow head and Rudolph Valentino eyes. Nearby were *two* Blue-winged Teals. I set down my camp stool and waited for more miracles. Vaux's Swifts skimmed the water for a drink. A Cliff Swallow came by to scoop up a beakful of mud to build its nest. There is a colony of Cliff Swallows under the eaves of the athletic building near the shellhouse, and this one undoubtedly was a member. Meanwhile, two male Mallards chased a female in an aerial display of flashing greens and browns. Was she testing them to see who was worthy of her favor? Was she wishing the dumb males would leave her alone? I decided I'd better watch awhile to try to find out.

I stayed from 8:00 a.m. to 4:00 p.m. Altogether, I walked more than three miles and saw 53 different species of birds. When I finally did get home, I was way too tired to mow the lawn. I flopped down in my Barcalounger and gave a deep sigh of fulfillment. My husband looked over at me. "How about stretching your legs?" he asked. "Want to go to the Fill?"

One year, my neighbor decided to remodel her house. She had a storage company unload a ginormous green bin in the middle of her yard so she could store all her stuff in it while the builders worked. The builders took much longer than she had thought, and the bin stayed in her yard for nearly two years. All her grass died. Hardy weeds grew up in clumps amid piles of rocks and bare earth.

I loved that yard. For two solid years, I didn't have to do a thing to my own yard in order to meet my low standard. The other neighbors never said a word of complaint about her yard. After all, she was remodeling. I wonder how much she paid to rent that bin.

13. Possibilities

Birding is all about possibilities. When you slam the door of your car in the parking lot and set out on Wahkiakum Lane, loaded down with your binoculars, your camp stool, a water bottle, maybe a scope and tripod slung across your shoulder, you never know what you'll find around the bend. The heavy tripod might dig into the acromioclavicular joint of your shoulder and excavate a hole there where no hole was ever meant to be, but you can ignore that. In fact, you don't even notice it. Why? Because anything might be awaiting you at the Fill.

It could be a mega-rarity, a bird from faraway Siberia or exotic Japan. Birds do fly, you know, and they can end up anywhere, so why not the Fill? Or you could discover some secret behavior that you never saw before, transforming even the most common bird into a rara avis. The Fill is a universe of possibilities.

One April morning, I was down at East Point, looking at two Pied-billed Grebes in the Cove. Pied-billed Grebes are one of the most common birds at the Fill. They are nondescript divers who look like brown ducks with pointy beaks, although they are not ducks at all. Pied-billed Grebes are actually more closely related to flamingos. Unlike their more flamboyant relatives, however, Pied-billed Grebes don't catch the eye. Their plumage is a low-key combination of gray-brown tones somewhere between soot and mud. In the spring, when other birds deck themselves out in bright colors, Pied-billed Grebes barely change at all—a little black under the chin, a black stripe around the bill, and that's about it.

The behavior of Pied-billed Grebes is just as low-key. Where Bald Eagles stoop dramatically on prey that frantically tries to get away, the Pied-bill Grebes paddle calmly around on the lake and ponds, occasionally diving for fish. Sometimes instead of dipping headfirst into the water, they squeeze out the air trapped in their feathers and slowly sink like a submarine. The operative word here is "slowly." Pied-billed Grebes lack the bon vivantness for drama. Occasionally, they might vary their submarine trick by not submerging all the way. On those occasions, their heads just break the surface like periscopes.

I must admit that I do enjoy watching them do this, but it's not exactly like they turn themselves into U-boats about to fire off torpedoes at some battleship steaming in for the kill. No, the grebes just drift along peacefully, gazing out at a very ordinary world. It's all so mild. Even their submarine behavior, once seen, is no more remarkable than a crow striding along a path or a starling pecking in the grass. Ho-hum.

So it was with only passing interest that I noticed the Pied-billed Grebes doing their grebeous thing out in the Cove this day. Not that I wasn't glad to see them. On the contrary, I play a little game with myself every time I go to the Fill. I tell myself I can't go home until I've seen at least 20 different species. I've been playing this game for nearly a quarter century. It's a way of keeping track of the species diversity at the Fill. In my game, a Pied-billed Grebe counts just as much as a rarity, so I was happy to see two of them near the cattails that border the Cove. They were number 15 on my way to 20.

Then I noticed that these two grebes were behaving oddly. They had stretched out their stubby necks as far as they could reach, and they were circling each other slowly, keeping their bills together. They looked like a living compass, drawing a circle on the still water—their bills were the point, their tails the pencil-line. I realized that the grebes were doing their mating dance, a sight seen rarely by most birders, and by me never before.

At first as I watched them, I thought, "Well, isn't that just typical." Not for the Pied-billed Grebe the demented mating dance of their larger cousins, the Western Grebes, who line up side by side, point their beaks into the sky, and levitate themselves off the water's surface, thrashing across a pond like whirligigs in a hurricane. No, this was a dance in slow motion, as nondescript as the birds themselves. But the longer I watched, the more interested I became. I began to perceive that the grebes were engaged in a stately minuet, a dance filled with elegance and grace. I was transfixed. I had never realized that Pied-billed Grebes could be so riveting.

Possibilities.

One of the dangers of getting old is that you can lose your belief in the possible. When you think of doing something new, you begin to tote up the risks and costs. All too often, the costs seem to outweigh the benefits, and the risks aren't worth it. Or you begin to see that in the long run, you can't win because the house always owns the edge, so why bet at all? Or you realize how much effort a given task is going to take because you've done it enough times before to know, and it all seems too much. So you end up spending more and more time sitting in the Barcalounger with your feet up and your sense of adventure on the wane.

People in our culture envision aging as an unwelcome process because it inevitably reduces possibilities. Once you hit adulthood, say the Peter-Panophiles of our culture, the rest is just a long, slow skid downhill to the end. At some point, you realize that you are never going to be president of the United States, even though when asked at age five, you were sure you could be, if you felt like it. At age five, the future opened up before you like an infinite cone, spreading wider and wider the further out you looked. As an about-to-be senior citizen, though, for me that cone is now reversed. I myself stand at the widest part of the cone. Ahead lies an ever-narrowing future, the realm of regret for the never-to-be.

Scientists used to believe that once we became adults, our brains stopped growing new neurons. When the old cells got too tired, they just winked out and there went another memory, or a thought, or an idea. No wonder we 50-somethings can't remember why we entered a room, or where we put our glasses. Better sit down in the Barcalounger for awhile.

But it's not true. We now know that the brain never stops growing new cells, if you encourage it. New ideas never stop coming, if you let them in. The possibilities never disappear, unless you banish them yourself.

My friend Aki Kurose was the world's exemplar of the possible. She taught first grade at Laurelhurst Elementary School for many years. For her, the possible was always within reach.

Aki used to take her students outdoors and line them up in one large group. Then she would send two kids skipping off to one side, then two more, and so on until the one big group had divided into many groups of twos. After that, she would have the kids start all over again, only this time in groups of threes. It was Aki's way of teaching the kids long division. It didn't matter that the public school curriculum waited until the fifth grade to teach long division—Aki believed in the possibility that her first-graders could understand such mathematics perfectly well.

When she was in her 70s, Aki developed terminal breast cancer. She fought it very hard and kept teaching until her body just wouldn't allow her to drag herself to work every day. Even after she retired, she volunteered to teach reading whenever she felt well enough. When even that became too much, Aki finally went home to stay.

I paid her a visit one day, thinking to cheer her up. I should have known better. Aki didn't need cheering up. She needed help tearing open a big box.

"What's in here?" I asked, helping her open it.

"It's my new computer," she said. Aki had retired shortly before the school library had been given a new computer lab. Computers were just beginning to appear as regular tools in the school's curriculum back then, and Aki had been very disappointed that she was leaving education just as this new technology was being adopted.

"Aki, why did you buy yourself a new computer?" I asked, thinking about how she had recently told me that the doctors had given her only a few more months to live.

"Well, Connie," she said, as though this should be obvious to

even the dimmest bulb, "nowadays everyone should know about computers, don't you think?"

I left her studying the manual. She told me that her next step was to get a modem so she could go online. I wasn't really surprised. For Aki, the idea of being connected to the whole wide world would be far too appealing to resist.

Possibilities.

Cancer did conquer Aki some months later, but fear of the unknown never did. Regret never did. Not for her the pinched, stingy, apprehensive vision of the future. For Aki, the world was filled with infinite, exciting possibility.

Birding gives me the same infinity. I never know what I'll see around the next corner. And there always is another corner that lies ahead. It draws me forward, into the rainbow and beyond, into a future where anything can happen.

A few weeks after I saw the grebes dancing in the Cove, I returned to Union Bay to find a little flotilla of baby grebes paddling in the wake of their parents. There was nothing ho-hum or nondescript about these babies. Their heads were striped black and white like zebras. A dramatic chestnut slash accented their napes. Their bills were a pastel pink, wide open and peeping in hunger.

No longer were the adults parading slowly like floats on the bay. No time for that anymore. While one stayed on the surface guarding the babies, the other adult was underwater hunting for fish. No sooner was one baby filled than another demanded something to eat. Who knew that grebes could hunt so fast, or be so endlessly fascinating? The ordinary had transformed itself into the extraordinary.

In the world of birding, such surprises are always possible. So, too, in all our worlds.

14. The Song of the Sparrow

This morning I heard a Fox Sparrow singing from the bushes east of the Dime Lot. It was a male with a very sweet song of trills and whistles. His song assured me that spring is here, no matter how cold the weather or how gloomy the skies.

I don't often encounter Fox Sparrows at the Fill anymore, not since the Center for Urban Horticulture (CUH) began its blackberry-clearing activities. Fox Sparrows used to come here in good numbers every winter. They would hunt for food by scratching in the leaf litter near blackberry thickets. Whenever danger threatened—which was often, at least in the minds of these cautious birds—the sparrows would pop into the nearest bush and disappear for the duration. I used to love to try to creep up on them as they foraged. If I managed to observe them without scaring them into hiding, I would award myself a gold star for my birding skills. I've missed doing that in recent years.

Mind you, I support getting rid of invasive species such as the Himalayan Blackberry, but there's no denying that ridding the Fill of blackberry bushes also rid us of many sparrows. That's why, after so many years of fox-less mornings, it was good to know that a Fox Sparrow thinks the Fill is habitable again. To me, it's a sign that although people can sometimes mess up the world, people can also fix it. The CUH people, you see, didn't just remove the nonnative brambles that were taking over the entire site. They replaced them with native shrubs, trees, and grasses. They hope that native wildlife such as the Fox Sparrow will move back once the land has become fruitful for them again.

I know that the Earth is in trouble from habitat destruction, and I also know that many species of birds have suffered precipitous declines. But rather than allow myself to sink into gloom about everything that's wrong, I prefer to focus on the things that are going right. I find this more inspiring. For me, inspiration leads to motivation, and motivation leads to action. The opposite is also true. Hopelessness leads to despair, and despair saps all energy.

Maybe that's why we humans are sometimes afflicted by depression and unhappiness. Those are functional feelings, in a backhanded way, because if you feel sad and depressed, then you can tell yourself it is wise to hunker down and wait for the clouds to go away. No use going out into the *Sturm* until it has passed you by, otherwise, you're far too likely to encounter the *Drang*.

Sturm und Drang is a German phrase usually defined as "storm and stress." However, the German word *Drang* can also mean impulse or urgency. That's really where the challenge comes in. If you feel an urgent need to do something, then you've got to sail out of your safe haven and act. Action requires commitment, energy, and time, all resources that may be completely depleted by ordinary life. Action is also risky. You might set your mind to accomplish something and fail. People might notice. It's safer to keep those sails furled and the anchor safely resting on the bottom of your personal sea. Perhaps there will be a Cousteau show on TV tonight, and you can venture out virtually.

I first noticed in myself this impulse to play it safe when I was in a badminton game in graduate school. I had played varsity badminton for many years and was pretty good, if I do say so myself. In this particular game, I was playing against a guy from China who could smash a shuttlecock so hard he would occasionally break his racket. Not only could he hit hard, but he was canny, too. Just when I would think he was going to take my head off with one of his smashes, he would waft a drop shot barely over the net that would float to the floor like a dandelion seed suddenly bereft of any breeze.

Usually when this happened, I would lunge from the back of the court, stretching out my racket while performing a dive worthy of an Olympic sprint swimmer. Nine times out of ten, my racket would meet only empty air. But every once in a while, I would return his shot and catch him off guard.

Well, on this day, my Chinese friend performed his classic drop shot, and I found myself rooted in the back of the court. I remember thinking, "I'll never be able to reach that shot, so I might as well not try." And I didn't.

I've thought about that moment many times since. I don't like it. It doesn't fit my self-image. I think of myself as a fighter who never gives up. "Life can knock you down, but it can never defeat you as long as you just keep getting up," I like to say. I also like to quote Ricky Young, a famous Washington surfer: "If you do nothing, nothing happens; if you do something, something happens." Clearly, doing nothing in that badminton game had indeed produced nothing but defeat.

As I've thought about that over the years, I have come to realize that any time we engage in a fight, the most important weapon we have is our attitude. In the fight to preserve natural habitat, we must believe that we can win. We must have hope in the future, and in our ability to shape that future for the good of the planet.

In 2004, my husband and I attended the grand opening of the Science Fiction Museum down at the Experience Music Project in Seattle Center. John, my very own mad scientist, was an invited VIP at the grand opening because he had earlier given a boffo talk about quantum mechanics to the sci-fi writers gathered in downtown Seattle for the Nebula Awards (sci-fi's equivalent of the Oscars). John was the token scientist at the awards dinner. His talk went over so big that the Powers That Be thought he should be an honored guest at the museum opening, too.

So that night we strolled down the red carpet leading into the museum, while local television and newspaper reporters filmed us on the off chance we might be important. Granted, they couldn't recognize us at the moment, but they figured that they might be able to ID us later when they looked in their field guides. The reporters were clustered thickly along the sidewalk so that all the museum guests had to pass in review in front of them, klieg lights glaring. John called it the perp walk.

Inside, we ran into some famous sci-fi writers and movie stars. Along with the writers and stars were hordes of fans, many of whom had dressed for the occasion. By "dressed," I mean they were costumed to look like aliens.

My favorite cosmic cross-dressers were an elderly couple wearing short capes, tights, and huge globes atop their heads. The globes were adorned with flashing colored lights that caught the eye and dropped the jaw. You don't expect to see senior citizens arrayed like that. I liked these aliens better than the two walking haystacks, who rustled ominously while they tried to balance batons stuck upright on top of their heads. Why batons? I couldn't say. I wanted to ask them, but I was too shy. I didn't know where their faces were, and I didn't want to commit a faux pas by addressing the backs of their heads, assuming they had some.

Now, you might think that all these people had alit upon the narrow end of the bell curve when it comes to goofiness. And you would be right. But looking deeper, you would also have to see something else, something profoundly important: these people were expressing a gentle love for "the other" and a serious commitment to the idea that the future, when we do finally encounter other life forms, will be bright and beautiful.

Is it naïve to believe in that future? I say no. If you want to have some control over the kind of future you will live in, then you have to be able to envision a future that you are inspired to work for and make come true.

As Martin Luther King, Jr., said in a speech in Atlanta at the tenth anniversary convention of the Southern Christian Leadership Conference, "When our days become dreary with low hovering clouds of despair, and when our nights become darker than a thousand midnights, let us remember that there is a creative force in this universe, working to pull down the gigantic mountains of evil, a power that is able to make a way out of no way and transform dark yesterdays into bright tomorrows."

King was speaking of God as that creative force, but ordinary human beings have the power to be a creative force as well. I have great faith in the resourcefulness and creativity of my species. I believe it is possible for us to bring all our diverse talents together to make our dreams come true. One of the most important dreams is to keep the environment healthy.

My faith in a bright future rests on the premise that much of what we do that affects the world lies within our power to choose. We have the power to choose wisely. The people who capped the Montlake Landfill 40 years ago and laid some topsoil over the clay made a choice to turn waste into wonderland.

It hasn't been easy to keep that dream alive. The commitment to restore native habitat is huge and expensive, and not just in terms of money. For years, I volunteered to pull out Purple Loosestrife— a noxious, foreign weed choking the Main Pond—so I know how much work it takes. It's not like you can complete the job and walk away, either. Invasive plants have sown their seeds abundantly in the soil, and they come back every year. Like doing the laundry, you may finish a load one day, but you know the next day, there will be more dirty clothes to wash. Still, you've got to keep at it; otherwise the dirty laundry will build up to mountainous proportions.

There are successes. A few years ago, the restoration ecology students cleared out a patch of brambles near the Dime Lot and planted quick-growing native maples, serviceberries, and other shrubs. Tenderly, they encased each new sapling in a blue plastic tube to protect it from rodents. By the time they were done, they had created a whole forest of blue tubes. They completed the project by putting in some dead snags and a few old logs to add cover, perches, and food.

This young grove has become very popular. Sparrows and finches keep up an almost continuous din as they chirp from one branch to another, seeking seeds. Flocks of Bushtits swirl through, searching for tiny insects. Tree Swallows nest here in little wooden houses supplied by the CUH. And one day in spring, a Merlin paid a visit, perching briefly on one of the snags. It was the same month I heard the Fox Sparrow sing.

Standing there, in the midst of such a victory, I wished I could take all those sci-fi people by the hand who had been at the museum on opening night, and lead them to the edge of that little grove. I would ask them to be silent and listen. Perhaps they would hear the music of one lone sparrow, who thinks the Fill is habitable again. Perhaps, if they were still, the Merlin would feel safe enough to wing in and perch above them, seeking a vole in the tall grasses nearby.

Perhaps then the people would be filled with the awesome beauty that is our Earth, and perhaps they would realize that working to preserve it is the greatest adventure of all. You don't need to travel to another galaxy to enter a different world. You don't need to read fiction to be the hero who saves the planet. There's a world to be saved right here on our doorstep.

15. A Secret World

Few people would say the Southwest Pond near the Dime Lot is beautiful. It's ringed with dead snags piled higgledy-piggledy like a giant's game of Pick Up Sticks. There is plant life here, but the plants all look vaguely ill. No current disturbs the scummy water, although every so often a bubble of methane from the decaying garbage underground breaks the surface.

At first glance, the methane bubbles are the only sign of life here. And yet this pond is stuffed with birds. It is a sanctuary for the species that prefer to hide from human eyes: the rails, herons, shorebirds, and warblers that conceal themselves in dense cover when people come around. Here on this pond, the birds seem to think they are safe from human interference. It is an Eden where they can do their birdly business.

There is one place where the Loop Trail swings close to the pond, and you can peek into this secret world. If you creep along the trail quietly and sit down on your camp stool, the birds take note but do not object. You have entered their home, and they will let you stay as long as you are still.

I did that today, one of those perfect days in May when the sky is Wedgwood blue, and puffy clouds change shape in the breeze. I wanted to check on the baby Pied-billed Grebes that hatched a week or two ago. Last time I saw them, the mama grebe had just caught a fish and was offering it to the first baby in line. Perhaps the mother grebe was a tyro, because the fish she had caught was much too big for the baby to swallow. The poor baby did its best, but it just

couldn't take it in. So the mama approached the second baby and tried to stuff in the fish. No good. Undeterred, she went to the third baby and tried. Still no luck. The baffled mother dropped her fish and picked it up again, perhaps to show the babies how easy it was to handle. The babies watched intently, but all the wishing in the world was not going to make their mouths any bigger or that fish any smaller.

Meanwhile, a Great Blue Heron landed on one of the dead stumps poking up from the pond. It immediately became a frozen statue of blue, white, gray, and chestnut. Only its mad yellow eye moved as it searched for fish to stab. Slowly, it lowered its head and cocked itself. I watched very closely because I knew that a Great Blue Heron has a special kind of neck. It's configured rather like a spring under tension. When the heron lets fly with its bill, the spring-loaded neck rockets the bird's bill forward, spearing any fish that's been foolhardy enough to get close. The motion is too fast for the eye to follow, but I always try.

The heron's muscles tensed. It lowered its bill a little more. I tensed up, too, ready for the stab. Instead, the heron raised one foot and began meditatively scratching its white, fluffy chin. It looked like an old geezer stroking his whiskers on the front porch in preparation for a tirade about how young folks are rude and the world is going to hell in a hand basket. All the heron lacked was a corncob pipe.

I shifted my binoculars a little, scanning for other denizens. My eye was caught by a pair of bright yellow legs standing on the shore. A Green Heron. Green Herons are small cousins of the great blues. Despite the name, they aren't really very green—they have a greenish cap, green-gray back, and rich mahogany cheeks and neck. They're perfectly colored to match the shadowy greens and browns of the pond edge. Green Herons don't like to be looked at. If they notice they're being watched, they'll either fly away or turn their backs on the observers. When they turn their backs, they become practically invisible against the vegetation.

This one, however, didn't realize I was there. It was too busy stalking frogs on the shore to notice me sitting nearby. In slow motion, it lifted first one foot, then the other. It took fifteen minutes to move one meter. English has no word for this kind of walk. Creep, mosey, amble, plod, toddle, dawdle—none of these verbs do justice to the glacial pace of this bird.

Just as the heron was about to take another step, a pair of joggers came running past on the trail. I looked up to see them go by, and when I turned back, the heron was gone. No matter. I knew it was still on the pond and would be back hunting frogs as soon as it thought the coast was clear.

I sat absorbing the stillness. The sky was a zoological garden of clouds. Once many years ago, I met a couple who were wandering around the Fill, looking high up in the sky all the while. I asked them if they'd seen any good birds, but it turned out they weren't birders. They were cloud collectors. They traveled the world collecting clouds the way other people collect Hummel plates. When I asked them how one collects clouds, they hauled out a small photo album and began telling me stories about the clouds they had seen. None of the photos were labeled. The collectors remembered each one and the story behind it. Their conversation was filled with, "Oh, do you remember this one at..." and "Ah, we were climbing Mt. Such and Such for this one." I think of them whenever I see spectacular clouds at the Fill.

As I was admiring a particularly swishy set of mare's tails, I saw a slight motion out of the corner of my eye. I turned my head and there it was: a Virginia Rail coming out to forage in the mud along the edge of the cattails.

Virginia Rails are prehistoric-looking birds with long bills and almost no tails. They live among the reeds and have the ability to thin themselves so that they can slip between clumps of cattails. If Green Herons are shy of people, Virginia Rails are positively misanthropic. Any day you see a Virginia Rail is a great day.

I stopped breathing, but it was no use. The rail had seen the slight turn of my head and was already heading back into the reeds, though luckily not in any hurry. Deliberately, it lifted one long-toed foot, then another. Just before it disappeared, it looked back over its shoulder at me. It gave me one glance, almost a wink, and then with a flick of its tiny tail, it was gone.

Every now and then, the Fill grants me such otherworldly moments that I feel like I am leaving the confines of the Earth. Oh, not my body. That lumpen mass stays anchored to the globe with human chains—bills to pay, a dentist's appointment to keep, and an oil change my husband insists the car needs, although the old oil still seems perfectly good to me. No, I mean that part of myself that imagines, the part that creates and believes in a universe beyond the senses. The ancient Egyptians called this part of us the *ba*, the spirit that is still human and fully alive in the here and now and yet can fly between this world and the next. They pictured the *ba* as a bird with a human head.

The Egyptians postulated an underworld as richly endowed with geography and culture as the known world, but I can imagine even more kinds of worlds, worlds that may exist in the future or the past or maybe never at all, except in my imagination. There really is no limit. I guess that's why people sometimes call imagination "flights of fancy." Maybe that's also why people have always loved to watch birds—because they can fly but so can we, at least with our minds. (Machine-aided flight is not the same.)

Whenever I see a Virginia Rail—so beautiful, breathing with the air of the prehistoric and hence the timeless—or when I share with the Great Blue Heron its hunt for fish, I feel my spirit spiral into the blue ether and merge with nature itself.

We humans have done our best to separate ourselves from nature. Nature is often too cold, too wet, too dirty, too dangerous. It's too real for many of us, and so we like to put some distance between us and it. But when we do that, we sever our connection to the living planet. It is a great loss.

Recapturing that feeling of connection, if just for a moment, transforms my life from the humdrum into the sublime. And that is why a muddy pond with beige scum and dead trees is beauty come to life for me.

16. No More Pishing

I am swearing off pishing. Pishing, for all you non-birders, means making a certain sound to call in birds. You purse your lips, expel a "P" sound, and follow with a long shushy noise. To our ears, it sounds like someone trying to imitate a cozy radiator, "Psshhh." But a foot or two away, it sounds just like the calls that a variety of songbirds make when they want to vocalize without actually singing. If other birds hear you pishing, they often pop up to see who's infringing on their territory.

My son Alex, a very strict birder, has castigated me in the past for calling in birds. He believes that a birder should have the skills to spot a bird where it is and how it is—no human manipulation. For him, calling in birds is the same as compromising the rules of any game. You cheat yourself by stacking the deck in your own favor, and that diminishes the fun.

There is a larger issue at stake, however, which has to do with how you think people should treat nature. Whether you're a religious person who believes in the biblical premise that God gave man dominion over the animals, or whether you're a secular evolutionist who thinks that the critter at the top of the food chain (i.e., *H. sapiens*) gets to eat whatever it wants, there is no denying that people have altered the landscape of the planet, and not just in modern times. Archaeologists are finding evidence that even nomadic hunters and gatherers from eons ago consciously set fires to clear vast areas of prairie so that it would be easier to hunt large, tasty herbivores.

Nowadays, our ability to alter the environment has greatly expanded. Global warming is just one example. There are many others. Explorers report that our plastic garbage can be found in the remotest marine environments. The sulfate aerosols from China blanket the entire globe. Acid rain in the Northeast is poisoning lakes and streams and will continue to have adverse effects for decades.

It's a long and dismal list that indicts us as caretakers. We have the power to affect habitat, and we seem to exercise it most exuberantly in the cause of materialism and destruction. This is not sustainable. As our need to consume resources expands, the natural world contracts. A study released on June 14, 2007, by the National Audubon Society reports that several of our most common birds are no longer very common—populations of some of our most familiar songbirds have declined as much as 80 percent. These declines are increasingly exacerbated by the effects of global warming. Stressed populations of birds have less and less ability to adapt to the rapid changes they are experiencing in their homes.

One conclusion I reach when I hear this kind of news is that we need to reduce our own impact on local habitat however we can. For me, this means in part that when I go out into the wild, I must remember that I am leaving my comfortable home behind. Instead, I am entering the domain of animals that are struggling hard to make it in a world that we have made much smaller for them. I need to be aware that I should behave as a good guest should and not make a pest of myself.

That's really why I've gone along with Alex's strictures. I don't play tapes of bird songs to attract males defending their territory (result: very short owl life list). I don't use the squeaker things you can twist to make a noise that arouses the curiosity of skulking songbirds (result: sparrow list could use some work). And I haven't learned to toot like a pygmy owl to call in the kinds of birds that would mob such a predator (result: warbler list needs beefing up).

On the other hand, pishing has always seemed innocuous to me. It's so very similar to what the birds hear normally in their homes all the time. It's just pleasant conversation, not loud, offensive music that would make a bird want to take a figurative broom and bang on the ceiling to shut me up. And besides, I can pish when Alex's back

is turned and he can't be certain I'm the one making that noise. At least, that's what I've told myself over the years.

No more. I'm quitting the pishing game. Going cold turkey. Sticking to the cardinal virtues. Starling behavior. Why? Because I just can't take the guilt anymore, not after today.

I was sitting under the crab apple tree down near East Point this morning, waiting for the birds to show up. This is a good place to watch the treeline that borders the cattails at the north end of Union Bay. I've often seen warblers, vireos, phoebes, and flycatchers here, and my hopes were high for a rarity. (Well, my hopes are always high for that.) Anyway, no birds were showing up at all, not even the usually ubiquitous crows. A single dragonfly came by, sat on a leaf for a moment, and then disappeared, leaving me alone.

Sitting there under the tree, with nothing in sight, the temptation crept upon me. Why not try a little pishing? Surely a little pishing wouldn't disturb the birds' normal behavior, would it? Pishing doesn't carry very far, so curious birds don't have to waste their energy flying in to see what's up, do they? Food is abundant this time of year, so bothering the birds with the tiniest, whispery pish wouldn't hurt them, would it? Alex is in California now, 800 miles away. What he doesn't know won't ruffle his feathers. Besides, purity is for the young and idealistic. We older folks know that the world of ethics is not black and white but filled with shades of gray.

Right?

Well, I pished. And I pished. Nothing. I could almost hear Alex's voice in my mind saying, "See, I told you not to do that." Then I got this eerie feeling that someone was watching me. I looked guiltily around, thinking a disapproving birder might have tiptoed up behind me. Nope. I still had the feeling, so I kept scanning. Not 30 feet away, perched on a bare branch was a huge Cooper's Hawk, one of the biggest and most beautiful I have ever seen. My eyes bugged out on stalks like a snail's.

The hawk was eyeing me in a most peculiar manner. I suspect that when I pished so loudly, she was called in, thinking the avian equivalent of, "Wow, this has got to be the biggest, fattest towhee or thrush or who-knows-what that I ever struck in my puff." Only to arrive and see me. I have a feeling that the hawk was overjoyed at first, thinking her ship had truly come in. But then, studying the situation, she must have begun to realize that bagging a prey as big as I presented certain logistical problems—problems that in the end were just too big to overcome. I think I must have met the hawk's eyes just at the moment when she realized that she was going to have to give me a pass.

If birds could sigh, this one would have let out a gusty one. A wave of guilt flooded my brain. Who needs a disapproving son staring gimlet-eyed right through me when a hawk can do the job just as well?

If you've ever been on the receiving end of a bird's look that was as reproachful as this one, you'll understand why I say that from now on, my lips are sealed. I am on the pishing wagon.

Part III

Summer

17. The Wild and the Tame

I seldom feel like throwing a rock at a bird. I believe that when one goes birding, one enters the birds' home, and thus one has an obligation to behave like a good guest. One should be polite and respectful, quiet and clean. Above all, one should not chuck rocks at one's host.

One day in July, though, sorely tried my philosophy and my patience. It all started when I got up before dawn in order to look for two reclusive rails, Virginia Rails and Soras. Both live most of their lives out of sight in the marsh. They don't like people and usually sneak deeper into cover when anyone appears. I have heard both species calling this year, and I suspect they're breeding in the cattails bordering the Southeast Pond. I figured that since it was late July, the moms might be out foraging with their babies, who would be too clueless and too hungry to rush back into hiding right away.

I arrived just after dawn. The weather was overcast and still. The usual traffic noise from the Floating Bridge across the lake was muffled and distant. No joggers or dog-walkers were circling the Loop Trail as yet to scare off the birds. Perfect conditions for seeing rails. How could I miss?

I should have known it wasn't going to be that easy. While I was fumbling around in the car for my gear, a campus security car pulled into the parking lot that serves both the Fill and the Center for Urban Horticulture. I straightened up and watched as a cop got out to question me. Several years ago, some eco-terrorists set fire to the CUH buildings, in the mistaken belief that a scientist there was doing recombinant DNA experiments with poplars. Since then, campus security has kept a close watch on the building. Seeing a scruffy figure hauling equipment out of a car at dawn must have set the cop's alarm bells ringing.

I don't know about you, but whenever I'm accosted by the authorities, I immediately feel guilty. My brain starts running through its card catalog of things I might have done wrong. The more it comes up empty, the more frantic the cortex becomes. I get flustered, and then I start babbling.

So it was with heart in mouth that I faced the campus security cop at the Fill. It wasn't long before I was in full babble, going on about rails, the breeding season, hasn't it been a cold spring, and what about those Mariners. I knew that arson was on the cop's mind, so it was only by some miracle that I didn't start talking about the benefits of controlled burning on the regeneration of prairie grasses. Eventually, the cop got back in his squad car and drove off, although I could see him talking into his radio.

With a sigh of relief, I hurried down the trail before the cop could change his mind. The worst was over. Now for the rails.

I'm not a great believer in karma, but I do think that the world has a tendency to stay in balance. The Earth tilts toward the sun during one part of the year, and then it tilts away from the sun for the other part of the year. If you dig a canal between two lakes, the water from the higher lake rushes into the lower lake until the two are the same. Magnetism has a positive pole and a negative pole. You get the idea.

The ancient Egyptians were the first to codify this rule of nature. They conceived of the world as divided into two balanced wholes. Land, for example, came in two kinds: the Black Land (i.e., Egypt) and the Red Land (i.e., everywhere else). There was the east bank of the Nile, and there was the west bank. There was this world, and there was the netherworld. The sun spent the day traversing the living world and spent the night traversing the netherworld. The Egyptians even had a pronoun that meant "two." Everything for them was in balance.

As a trained Egyptologist, I guess I have soaked up that idea
until it permeates my own thinking. That's why if I have a miserable experience birding one day, I believe I'm due to have a great
experience the next day. If you chase halfway across the state to find
a mega-rare Bean Goose only to have it fly off into the ether before
you can set up your scope, well then, the next time an equally rare
Eurasian Kestrel appears in our state, you'll be the first to see it. This
is especially true because you missed the kestrel the last time it was
here and had to endure everyone's look of pity as they said those fell
words, "You should have been here yesterday."

Therefore, after my miserable experience with the cop at the Fill,
I figured all my efforts to find rails were about to be rewarded. It
was only fair.

Unfortunately, as I approached the pond, a lone Killdeer spotted
me and decided to announce my arrival to all the other birds within
a half-mile. Not just announce. The Killdeer placed himself a few
feet in front of me and proceeded to herald my arrival everywhere
I went. It was uncanny how he seemed to know when I was going
to turn off on a side trail and go down a different path. Staying just
ahead of my every step, the Killdeer called and called, like he was
the vizier leading a Pharaoh parade. "Make way for the Pharaoh!
The Pharaoh is in the building. Here comes the Pharaoh. Did you
hear me? *Make way!*"

That Killdeer was so loud and persistent that every other bird
stopped what it was doing to see what was up. At first, most of
the birds realized that it was just me, the odd duck in a blue hat
they've seen a hundred times before. The birds probably think I molt
into different plumage way too often, but they know I'm harmless.
The Killdeer has seen me many times, too, but he just wouldn't quit.
Eventually, all the birds decided that discretion was the better part
of valor, and they flew off—even the Mallards, who are so used to
people that when they see a person with bread, they come and beg
for food. Any rails in the vicinity were long gone.

The Killdeer must have realized he was alone at last. Looking
around and seeing no other birds, he finally shut his beak, eyed me

one more time, and then flew off, too. Good thing. I had just spotted a likely-looking rock.

Muttering under my breath about how I had missed the Bean Goose and the Eurasian Kestrel—not to mention the Eurasian Dotterel and many other rarities as well—so you'd think I deserved at least one Virginia Rail, I trudged back to the car. Might as well go home. On the way, though, I stopped off at the Cove to check out the Turtle Logs that line the north end. I've seen rails here in the past, and I hoped that some might still be willing to come out and do a line dance on the logs, despite the fact that the Killdeer's calls must have alerted them to danger. No rails—the Killdeer had seen to that—but I happened to glance over at a Pied-billed Grebe's nest among the lily pads.

Two of these compact little grebes have been nest-building here for about a week now. Their nest is only 30 feet from the shore. One of the parent grebes was scooching around on the nest, and I focused on it with my binoculars. I wanted to see its feet. You don't often get a chance to see a grebe's feet out of water because grebes almost never come out on land. They can't walk. Their feet are designed to swim. Grebes' feet are set back far back on their bodies. When grebes submerge to hunt for little fish, they turn their feet sideways and use them like flukes to power through the water. Grebes' feet are wonderfully designed for underwater speed, but out on land, they're almost useless. Instead of walking, grebes flop. Knowing how vulnerable they are on land, grebes come out of the water only to nest, so that's the best time to try to see their feet.

This grebe was turning around and around on its nest, moving something at its feet with its bill. At first, I thought the grebe had caught a fish and was trying to swallow it. Then I saw what it really was. Pecking out between its legs was its egg!

I caught only a momentary view of the egg, a dull white with speckles, then the grebe flopped down to cover it. After the grebe got settled, its mate brought a piece of plant to build up the nest a little more. Both parents touched bills with each other, and then the bird on the nest helped to tuck in the new plant strand.

As I sat there in wonderment, I realized that both the Killdeer and the grebes had given me the same gift: the sense that I shared the wildness of nature with them. The Killdeer had warned off all the other birds I wanted to see, and despite all my wishing, he would not shut up. I had no control over him. In the same way, the grebes were also out of my control. They didn't care that I was watching them as they went about their business. They did what Pied-billed Grebes have been doing for millions of years without the intervention of humans. And much as I hate to admit it, the fact that I missed all those rare birds had nothing to do with some crazy theory about how the world owes me, based on my personal misery index. I missed the birds because I had my schedule, but they had theirs.

Wilderness, says naturalist and poet Gary Snyder, is different from civilization in the sense that the wild is unconstructed. It isn't built by people; it grows by itself. "Wilderness," he writes, "is simply a place that has been left wild for a while. It doesn't have to be pristine. It doesn't have to be virgin. Everything will become wilderness again, sooner or later. Nature's resilience and inevitability mean that the universe is ultimately wild, just as we are surrounded by a vast wilderness called outer space."

According to Snyder, the essence of wilderness is that it is self-organizing. Wild doesn't mean disorganized or lawless. It does mean that humans do not supply the rules of the organization.

One of the greatest appeals of the Fill for me is this very fact. No human told those Pied-billed Grebes to build a nest among the lily pads. We humans did not hammer together a nest box for them. We did not raise a grebe by hand, and then place the grebe in the box we had made. No, the grebes built their own nest by their own efforts. Nor were the grebes in a zoo, where their schedule was controlled by us. They decided to breed in their own time, when they somehow judged there would be enough food to raise their young. The grebes fed themselves and did not wait for a handout from us.

Nature, as expressed by the grebes and Killdeer at the Fill, really is resilient. I find this thought comforting because it means that for all our power to destroy, nature has the power to survive.

At the same time, this resilience of the wild does not have to exist alone, without any human help. The Fill is a constructed place, a landfill turned into a nature study area by us humans. The Fill is living proof that there is plenty we humans can do to create habitat that might induce grebes to call it home. We can help, but we would do well to remember that helping is not the same thing as controlling. As a Seattle Academy history teacher, Robin Gage, once told me, "Perhaps we can teach ourselves to try to approach different places by sitting back and letting them show themselves to us rather than coming and imposing ourselves on them."

In an age when virgin wilderness—on land at least—has mostly disappeared, letting places show themselves to us means that we should allow the wild places to exist for the wild. The Fill is primarily a natural area reserved for the wild things; it is not a park made especially for the people.

The managers of the University of Washington's Center for Urban Horticulture, who are in charge of the Fill, make this distinction very well. You can see it with your own eyes. The wildness of the Fill appears among the rolling hills, where the brown grasses grow tall and the Savannah Sparrows build their nests completely hidden by the prairie. The wild can also be found among the cattails that ring the smaller vernal ponds, preventing humans from looking in and disturbing the birds. The wild also exists in the dense grove of trees growing around Leaky Pond near the start of the Loop Trail, a grove so dense no human knows what goes on inside.

The Fill is defined by these wild places, but it is not managed solely for wild creatures. Students' study plots dot the landscape. Near the CUH buildings, the land is cultivated as a garden. The grass is kept green and trimmed. Exotic flowers color the rockery with splashes of magenta, orange, and purple.

Sometimes, the CUH rents out a small amphitheater near here for weddings. The amphitheater is on the edge where wild meets tame. To the east are the rockery and the CUH buildings. To the west is the Fill. I often sit here in the early mornings and wait for the hummingbirds to hover near my head. They ignore me as they drink nectar from a serviceberry bush, mere inches from my face. The hum of their wings is a deep sound for their size.

When the wedding decorators show up and begin setting up rows of white chairs on the grass, the hummingbirds and I both retreat to watch from a distance. None of us will go near all the activity. We perch nearby and watch humans' attempts to organize all life. One time, the bride decided to ring the amphitheater with topiary bunnies, which gazed unseeingly at the empty white chairs. She tied a white ribbon around each bunny's neck—a perfect metaphor for how strong our desire can be to tame the wild and make it cute, i.e., ours. The wild is many things, but seldom cute.

Many people come to the Fill to enjoy the open spaces, and the CUH staff must do what they can to accommodate them. They maintain a gravel path that loops around the southern half of the

reserve, so people can stroll and jog. Every few hundred yards, the staff have allowed a dirt path to be trodden flat so people can get close to the water.

In the late summer, after the prairie birds have nested, the staff mows down the tall grass. They do this in part to control the foreign, invasive plants that would otherwise take over and displace the grasses. But there could be another reason, too—three years ago, a couple of kids foolishly shot off some fireworks and set fire to the prairie. I suspect the CUH director still gets heart palpitations when he thinks about where that fire could have spread. The surrounding neighborhood is loaded with million-dollar homes and politically well-connected people.

I have seen many people doing their thing at the Fill. Joggers trot around and around on the path as they do their laps, their ears plugged by iPods. More serious runners race around faster, the sweat streaming down their backs. People on their way to work or to school stride along Wahkiakum Lane, carrying backpacks and a sense of hurry. Dads and moms push baby-strollers. Some of the parents are two-fers: their babies are strapped in high-tech racing strollers so the adults can jog while the babies get their dose of fresh air. Dog-lovers walk their dogs on long leashes and, for the most part, heed the signs begging them to stay on the path. Students march around in clumps, their pens and notepads ready when their teacher points out noxious weeds. Fishers catch perch. Flautists practice.

Many people use the Fill, but the wild things live here. It is really their space. Our homes lie elsewhere, away from the elements that the animals can enjoy and sometimes must endure, whatever nature decrees. We humans come only to visit.

That is why I didn't pick up a rock to throw at the Killdeer who was spoiling my desire to see rails. My desire was unimportant, irrelevant even. I was not in my space. I was in the wild.

18. A Falcon's Value

Everyone perks up when a Peregrine Falcon comes to the Fill. The birders get excited because a falcon is a cool bird, one of the perennial favorites that we post onto the birding hotline whenever we spot it. The birds get excited for another reason: they might become the falcon's dinner. Falcons catch and eat other birds.

In the summer, you can always tell when a Peregrine is around because the swallows gather in a swarm and begin giving their alarm call. They are one of the few birds that can fly fast enough to pester a Peregrine. Other, slower birds behave like the scientist and his colleague in the famous joke. The two men were studying a pride of lions on the African savannah. The lions began to get agitated, and the big male of the pride looked like he was about to charge. The scientist noticed that his colleague had sat down and was putting on a pair of running shoes. "Are you crazy?!!" he asked his friend. "You can't outrun a lion."

"I don't have to," his friend replied, still tying on his shoes. "I only have to outrun you."

Many species of birds have adopted a similar strategy. When a Peregrine flies into a flock of Dunlins feeding on an ocean beach, for example, the Dunlins all leap into the air as one cloud. The Peregrine hunts above the cloud, driving it back and forth. As long as the Dunlins stay together, the falcon tends to hold back. But woe betide the sick or tired Dunlin who drops behind the flock. It immediately becomes the focus of the Peregrine's attack, rather like the slow-running scientist.

Sometimes the Peregrine stoops from high above its prey, swooping down with wings folded. At such times, it has been clocked at speeds greater than 200 mph. More often, though, once the Peregrine has identified the weakling in a flock, it homes in on it and begins a deadly chase. The Peregrine's keen eyes stay fixed on the twists and turns of its chosen target, while it powers up its long, pointed wings and simply outflies its victim.

One hot day, I was walking the Loop Trail when I heard the swallows start screeching overhead. Knowing a falcon might be nearby, I began to gyrate wildly, searching for the bird. And then I found it, perched on a bare, dead sapling a mere five yards from the trail: a juvenile, still showing some raggedy fluff. It was gazing down at the reeds below, looking for something to eat and ignoring the vocal swallows.

I set up my scope and looked at its fluffy head, a powder puff of feathers. "Aww, how cu...," I started to say. But before I could finish, the bird lifted its head and looked straight into my eyes. The word "cute" died aborning. There was nothing cute about this bird. Its fierce gaze was one hundred percent hunter, zero percent Bambi. It made me realize, for the millionth time, that birds are not really like us. Perhaps no animal is. Birds may share many basic impulses and biologies with us, but they do not share our spiritual core. Things that matter to us do not matter to them.

Well, of course, I can almost hear the scientists out there say, that's because birds' brains are much smaller than ours. They can't think at our level, can't imagine, can't reason. They use instinct to build things—their nests are nothing like the new Bird's Nest in Beijing, the Olympic stadium that wowed the world when it was unveiled in 2008. Birds lead simple lives. They hunt for food, mates, roosts, and nesting sites. They never heard of Nietzsche and wouldn't care about him if they did. Birds are members of the lower orders.

All true, and a complete reversal of how humans used to think about animals. Before science and technology came along, primitive humans found the natural world to be filled with mystery and magic. Animals could do many things that people could only dream of.

They could fly through the air, swim forever underwater, or run cross-country much faster than we. They could follow a scent trail, hear better, see farther. Animals were gods in the ancient days, and we revered them.

We do so no longer. At best, we love them now as lesser creatures, as pets or second-class beings that need to be taken care of. Even wild animals are becoming domesticated, or at least parkified. As the Earth fills up with more people and more development to accommodate our needs, we know that if we want to preserve the species that are still here now, we will have to become their custodians. Hence the parks, preserves, and zoos that dot our world.

Given these realities, what kind of custodians will we be? Will we be able to save everything? If not—and current trends indicate definitely not—then how will we triage the species worth saving? What criteria will we use to decide whether a species lives or dies?

So far, we have shown that we are not equal-opportunity stewards. We worry most about tigers, pandas, and other animals with a high cuteness factor. Some of us may extend this concern to animals with a lower cuteness factor—the Snail Darter, or the Ridge-nosed Rattlesnake—but for the majority of us to become engaged enough to preserve another species, we have to find something about that species that appeals to us directly. If not cuteness, then a species has got to have medical use, or it's got to look good when we wear it, or taste good when we eat it—anything that makes it valuable to us.

And who are we? The apex of creation, as both the Bible and Darwin would agree. Or so we would like to think.

I read somewhere that the part of our brain used to recognize human faces is larger than in any other creature. You can see how true this is by opening a bag of potatoes. Every potato is different, but no matter how long we gaze at one potato, if we look away and try to re-create it in our minds, it is quite a chore. We have to really struggle. Recognizing Grandpa's face, though—even if it does resemble a potato—is easy.

This trait—part of our profoundly and even compulsively human-centric consciousness—seems to drive us to put everything into human terms. Copernicus may have been correct astronomically; he was surely wrong psychologically. The sun *does* revolve around us, and so does everything else. Our egotism makes it hard for us to preserve habitat purely for the benefit of other critters. Better for us birders if we can find ways to put human value on such things.

Ornithologist Paul Kerlinger has long advocated that birders should carry business cards wherever we bird. On the card should be printed a statement: "I am a birder. I have come to this region because you have preserved great habitat that attracts birds. I am spending my money in your establishment because of that."

Kerlinger believes that attaching a dollar value to habitat will encourage us to preserve it, and, he points out, there is plenty of dollar value to attach. He estimates that many birders spend $1,500 per birding trip, and we take a lot of trips. The U.S. Fish & Wildlife Service estimated in 1992 that 100,000 birders a year visit Cape May, a famous birding spot in New Jersey near Kerlinger's home. Kerlinger reports that this number has increased every year. He also reports that Hawk Mountain, a raptor trap in Pennsylvania, attracts more than 70,000 birders a year. J. N. "Ding" Darling National Wildlife Refuge in Florida gets 750,000 visitors a year.

With that many birders visiting similar places all over North America and spending untold millions of dollars a year, says Kerlinger, local residents and business owners should be made aware of the wealth that lies on their doorstep. When they realize how lucrative it is to preserve habitat that attracts birds and hence birders, they will take good care of it as a resource.

Kerlinger is undoubtedly correct. We do live in a society that tends to evaluate the worth of almost everything in dollar terms. But much as I respect his idea and even follow his advice about telling locals why I'm spending money in their town, I don't like the fact that I belong to a society that believes price is the best way to value something. I could never put a price on the feeling I got when that young Peregrine gazed straight into my eyes, allowed me to see something truly alien, and made me understand that we may occupy the same planet, but we live in different worlds.

A Falcon's Value 105

That revelation, in turn, has made me think about how little we truly know about our environment. I mean, when my daughter rolls her eyes for the fiftieth time because no matter how hard she tries to teach me, I still cannot fathom how to make my new cell phone act as a text messenger (and I will probably never be able to bring myself to type "u r gr8"), then I know how little I understand the culture I live in. That culture is a small subset of the local ecology, of which Seattle is a part. The local ecology is a subset of a much bigger regional, and even planet-wide, ecology. How much of that ecology do we really understand at the deepest level?

Edward O. Wilson, an evolutionary biologist and professor at Harvard, says in his book, *Naturalist*, "The great majority of species of organisms—possibly in excess of 90 percent—remain unknown to science. They live out there somewhere, still untouched, lacking even a name. The greatest numbers are in remote parts of the tropics, but many also exist close to the cities of industrialized countries. Earth, in the dazzling variety of its life, is still a little-known planet."

If we all realize that, then perhaps we can approach the matter of altering ecology with a little more humility and a lot more caution. Perhaps we can also appreciate far more the ecology we already have and work harder to preserve it as it is, even if that does mean making a few sacrifices for the sake of other creatures who share the Earth with us. It is their planet, too, and we humans are not the center of the universe.

Pondering these humbling lessons, I went home, selected a potato that looked remarkably like Grandpa, and stuck it in the oven.

19. A Fill Fantasia

July at the Fill is when most of the baby birds who hatched here grow their flight feathers and leave the nest. Many of the babies still need their parents' care, though, or at least they think they do. They follow the parents around from point to point, begging for food. Whenever the parents alight, the babies crowd in close, crouch down, quiver their wings repeatedly, open their beaks, and cry. Whether eagles, sparrows, grebes, or finches, the babies' cries are piteous and horribly, horribly persistent. They simply won't shut up. If the parents had hair, they would be tearing it, no doubt.

Eventually, the parents manage to elude the babies, who, one hopes, have learned enough to fend for themselves.

One baby who seems to be doing well is the Bewick's Wren who is growing up at the Leaky Pond near the east entrance of Wahkiakum Lane. I call this area the Leaky Pond because years ago, the Center for Urban Horticulture folks built a pond here that leaked out all its water. There remains a drain optimistically raised about a foot above sea level, so to speak, but the drain has never been needed for flood control. A few puddles show up during a wet winter, but they are much too shallow for the drain to have any effect on them at all.

In the trail right by the drain, if you look very closely, you will see two little depressions. They were made by the Bewick's Wren and his sister (or perhaps brother—with Bewick's Wrens, it's hard to tell). The two babies come out in the afternoons to take dust baths here. They scrunch down into the trail, then motor around with their feet, tails stuck straight up and wings flapping till the dust clouds

rise overhead. They look like tiny hydroplanes, with rooster tails rising behind and a spray of dust-drops splashing at every turn. One of them was calling exuberantly as it bathed, that rattling, harsh, one-note call that sounds like a miniature jet turbine sputtering to get the hydroplane out of the slip and onto the lake. Eventually, the motor caught, and the wren flew off.

Today, the junior wren I call the punk rocker tried out his latest song. He reminds me of a punk rocker because he still has a few tufts of down sticking up on his head, like a teenager's mohawk, or maybe an emo mullet, or perhaps even dreads—anyway, some kind of rebellious style sure to make a mother weep.

Bewick's Wrens don't always sing—sometimes they squawk or call or chip—but when they choose to belt out an aria, they are one of the most musical of all birds. They have a big repertoire, which they like to individualize. Some of the virtuosos would put Plácido Domingo to shame. So varied are their songs that on the weekly "birding by ear" quizzes that I used to take in my Seattle Audubon master birder classes, whenever the proctor played a bird's song that I couldn't identify, I would write down, "Bewick's Wren." You'd be surprised how often that answer was correct.

Because the Bewick's Wrens' songs are so variable and do not seem to be predetermined by instinct, developing one's own song has got to be tough for each wren. At least, it has been for the punk rocker. He's been working on his song for about a week now. As do many music students, he started out by singing an abbreviated solfège, but he cut it off after only a few notes. Evidently, something was lacking. A few days later, he was singing a longer song, but I have to say it sounded rough and unmusical. I spied him in the bushes with his head thrown full back. He was giving it his all, but I'm afraid the critics, had there been any in the audience, would have panned him.

Today, though, he had a breakthrough. I was passing by his favorite bush when I heard the most beautiful, complicated song I have ever heard. I couldn't identify what bird was singing—something exotic, was my first thought, and then I realized: Bewick's Wren, of course. I stood still to listen. The song went on and on, with Bach-like variations on a theme. I tried to find the singer, but he was too well hidden. At last, he reached the grand finale and stopped. There was a little rustle of leaves, and a tiny, tufty head peeked out for an instant, then slowly withdrew. Bravo! Bravissimo! I waited there, hoping for an encore or at least a curtain call, but the maestro was done for the day. Why try to outdo perfection?

The Fill has given me many moments like this, when sound fills my ears—and through them, my soul—with beauty. The beauty is not always obvious. The Spotted Towhee who hangs out near the Wedding Rock, for example, sounds like a squeaky kitten. Gadwalls quack like Mallards with a head cold—not pretty. Great Blue Herons crank. Steller's Jays scold, a one-note tirade that verges on nagging. To me, they're all beautiful because when I hear these songs, melodious or un-, they lift me up and carry me to a different world.

To hear them properly, I have to be able to tune out the human noise that is ever-present in the city: cars whooshing over the Floating Bridge, the squeal of brakes as the frat boys do donuts in the Dime Lot, the choppa-choppa of the emergency helicopter bringing a child to the helipad for transport to Seattle Children's Hospital—the worst sound ever.

None of these human-made sounds are pleasant to the ear, even when they mimic nature. The whoosh of the traffic, for example, sounds a bit like the rush of a waterfall, but somehow the one is serene, the other stressful.

Earlier this year, there was a group of students making sound recordings at the Fill, using parabolic dishes and big microphones. One of the students had crept to the edge of Shoveler's Pond and was holding his mike out toward three Wilson's Phalaropes that were feeding near the shore.

Phalaropes are shorebirds with long legs and needlelike bills that they use to pick at the surface of mud or water as they hunt for insects and small crustaceans. These particular birds were in migration, on their way north to Canada or perhaps east across the Cascades to central Washington, where they breed in prairie wetlands. Two of the phalaropes were male, and one was female. Unlike the females of most bird species, the female Wilson's Phalarope is more colorful than the male. I suppose it's because Wilson's Phalaropes reverse gender roles to a great extent. The males make the nests; the females compete for partners. Once the females have laid their eggs, they leave the task of childcare to the males and head south.

It's not every year that I see a Wilson's Phalarope at the Fill. If one does show up at all, it comes in May or early June and stays only briefly. This was the first time I had ever seen three together, and it was quite a treat.

The sound teacher asked me if I would like to use her equipment to listen to the sound of the phalaropes' feet as they paddled and waded in the pond. "Oh, yes," I replied. Who would ever pass up the chance to hear phalarope feet?

I put the padded headphones on and heard thunder rumbling in the distance. Snatching off the headphones, I looked around wildly for the thunderclouds and lightning. Thunderstorms are very dangerous at the Fill, where you can easily be the tallest—and most electrically attractive—thing in the vicinity. But the sky was clear, and the teacher was laughing. "That's not thunder," she said. "It's the cars rumbling over the bridge."

A whole new kind of pollution I had not been aware of before. We've got air pollution, water pollution, light pollution, and now this. It would be easy to throw up our hands and say, "It's all too much." It would be easy to admit that we humans made this mess, but we can't change anything because the problems are too big. What can one person do?

In the 1950s, Jim Ellis, a bond attorney in Seattle, was searching for a civic project to contribute his time to. His younger brother Bob had been killed in World War II. To make some sense out of a senseless act of destruction, Jim Ellis and his wife Mary Lou decided they would devote a portion of the rest of their lives to improving the world in ways that Bob would have done if he had lived.

One of their first projects was the cleanup of Lake Washington. In those days, most of the towns that encircled the lake dumped their raw sewage directly into it. A few of the towns had sewage treatment plants, but the lake was overwhelmed by the towns that didn't. The lake became so polluted that "No Swimming" signs were posted on the beaches. The algae became so thick that it was said you couldn't see an eight-inch, bright-white dinner plate three feet below the surface of the water.

The Ellises banded together with a few other civic-minded citizens and came up with the idea of forming a supergovernment, a coalition of municipalities that would tackle a regional problem regionally. The creation of Metro—the Municipality of Metropolitan Seattle—was put on the ballot in March of 1958 and defeated. The people in the suburbs were afraid that Seattle, the "Octopus," would take over their own governments, so they voted it down.

Mary Lou suggested that if Seattle offered to buy some of the little sewage treatment lines that the suburbs had built, and if the suburban mayors could be seen to have suggested this, then perhaps they would get behind the measure. That's exactly what happened. In September of that same year, Metro passed.

"We turned Kirkland from a two-to-one 'no' vote to a two-to-one 'yes' in five months," said Ellis in an interview he gave to four of my middle-school writing students. "We did that with all the Eastside cities. We didn't win everywhere, but we passed it inside and outside Seattle. Metro cleaned up the lake one year ahead of schedule at a lower cost than had been advertised in the campaign, and received an All-America City Award, shared by all the cities in Metro."

There are many similar stories about people banding together, overcoming opposition, and using the power of the ballot box or the courts to achieve real political, social, economic, and environmental change. The Clean Air Act, the Endangered Species Act, the creation of national parks, the designation of wildernesses—none of these things were easy or quick. They happened because we are the one species on the planet that can make cultural decisions that can affect wide swaths of the natural world.

Metro is a perfect example. The creation of Metro was a cultural decision we made by voting to create a new form of government.

Metro, in turn, used taxpayer dollars to build a sewage treatment system that piped our waste to a plant we built in Discovery Park: another cultural decision. Lake Washington is no longer polluted: a natural outcome of our cultural acts.

Despite all the bad news about the environment, there is great news as well. The fact that so much of nature is at risk because of what we humans do means that we humans can also save much of nature because we can change what we do.

And why should we change? What is so great about nature?

Three nights ago, I sat near the Lone Pine Tree at dusk, hoping to see the Barn Owl that other birders had reported. As the sun sank and the light faded from gold to silver, the Barn Owl floated out of the trees north of the Main Pond. It coursed over the tall grass in the hollows, then flowed toward me on a long glide. As it passed within a few feet, it turned its white, heart-shaped face toward me and stared, zombie eyes looking out of a ghostly face. I could see every feather on its body, the colors mottled brown and bluish-gray above, white and brown below.

The owl's flight was perfectly silent, because owl wings have specially adapted fringing on the leading edges that makes the air rushing over the wings flow without any sound. I knew this intellectually, but that's not why I heard nothing. The Barn Owl's flapping could have been as loud as cannon fire and I would have heard nothing—I was too enthralled by vision alone. I know this to be true because all the traffic on the bridge, the frat boys in their muscle cars, the joggers crunching gravel, three other birders breathing a few inches away—they all drifted off into the fifth dimension. In the here and now, all was mute and still, even my heartbeat. There was only the owl.

Then the owl flew past, and the Earth resumed rotating. Not the same Earth, though. It had changed, become more magical, a place where time can stand still, where earth-bound sounds may stop but the harmony of the heavens does not. And where pure beauty flutters on wings of white.

20. A Pocket of Paradise

Magic happens at the Fill in the most unlikely places and at the most unlikely times. Take one day in August, for example. As I was walking the Loop Trail, I stumbled upon a natural blind on the southwestern edge of the preserve. There was a little trail in the cattails that grow thick here at the end of the trail, and I was curious to see what lay on the other side. I gently pushed back a waving spear of vegetation that brushed my face, set down my camp stool, spat out a mouthful of mosquitoes, and took a look.

What I saw was a perfect paradise of birds. Drifting among the lily pads like day-trippers drowsing on floating air mattresses were ducks galore: Mallards, Gadwalls, all three species of Washington teals (Blue-winged, Green-winged, and Cinnamon), Wood Ducks, and even a lone Northern Pintail. On a little mud island 20 feet from shore, American Coots and Canada Geese were preening their feathers, now and then stopping to exchange a neighborly honk or two. Shuttling around them were a number of shorebirds freshly arrived from Alaska on their way south: a Lesser Yellowlegs, several Least Sandpipers, a delicate Baird's Sandpiper, a spanking-white and gray Semipalmated Sandpiper, and a Spotted Sandpiper. They were busy foraging for insects, crustaceans, and worms, knowing they had to build up fat for the long flight south.

The Baird's Sandpiper was a particularly exciting find. Baird's Sandpipers breed north of the Brooks Range in Alaska and all along the northern edge of Canada, where land meets the Arctic Ocean. They spend the winter in South America, some flying all the way to

Patagonia. Most adults migrate through the center of our continent; the juveniles, a little more clueless, spread out and sometimes appear on the coast or in Eastern Washington. Seeing one on this day in the middle of the city, so far from any normal migration route, was a rare privilege. I was thrilled to note its elegant body, its long wings tapering to a point beyond its tail, each brown feather on its back meticulously outlined in white. It was a Chanel kind of bird mixed in with the more common Kmart Killdeers and ducks.

Altogether, there were 22 different species of birds in an area smaller than the average-sized McMansion. The birds all seemed very calm, despite the fact that dump trucks kept rumbling back and forth along the gravel road that borders the west side of the Lagoon. The University of Washington's Intercollegiate Athletics Department is building again, and the air is filled with sounds of construction. The dump truck drivers carrying dirt away from the site seemed oblivious to the wondrous birds just a step away—but then, the birds also seemed oblivious to the people.

It was a discombobulating juxtaposition of industrious human activity just 50 yards away from the peace and quiet of a Thoreauvian pond. I didn't know whether to be sad that human activity has decimated the natural landscape to the point where birds literally have to step over each other to feed; or whether to be glad that nature is robust enough that it survives in such profuse diversity.

My sadness is tempered by the fact that although humans mess up the world, humans can also fix up the world. My gladness is tempered by the fact that although the Fill hosts so much diversity, the number of individual birds is small. It's great to see a Spotted Sandpiper bobbing its rear end up and down while it stabs its beak to catch insects that fly up from the mud. But I saw only one Spotted Sandpiper today. Spotties used to breed here commonly. I felt thrilled to see the Baird's Sandpiper, but populations of northern-breeding sandpipers have plummeted in our lifetime.

The Fill is a mix of wild and domestic. The wild birds show up on their own schedule, uncontrolled by us. The landscape, though, is managed. Gardeners from the Center for Urban Horticulture and

UW students are constantly at work modifying the micro-habitats that characterize this place. Many of the modifications are restorative, designed to replace invasive foreign species with native ones. Some, however, are designed more with humans in mind: the demonstration gardens that exhibit ornamentals from all over the world, the sod experiments to help people's yards and golf courses. Whatever the purpose, the Fill feels the hand of *Homo sapiens* almost everywhere.

The Fill is not unique in this. According to a June 2007 *Science* magazine article, the whole planet is feeling the heavy weight of human interference. "As of 1995," write authors Peter Kareiva, Sean Watts, Robert McDonald, and Tim Boucher, "only 17 percent of the world's land area had escaped direct influence by humans, as indicated by one of the following: human population density greater than one person/square km; agricultural land use; towns or cities; access within 15 km of a road, river or coastline; or nighttime light detectable by satellite."

The authors go on to say that since for all practical purposes, all nature is or soon will be domesticated, we have to decide how we should manage this domestication successfully.

The authors define success by listing three paths to domestication: "Some paths of domestication will result in improved ecosystems both for people and for other species; other paths of domestication will result in ecosystems that are clearly better for humans but not for other species; and some paths of domestication will result in ecosystems that are too degraded to benefit people or other species."

I imagine the authors would choose "Door Number One." But nowhere on this list is any kind of domestication that would result in preservation of the wild purely for the sake of the wildlife, regardless of whether that benefits humans. Indeed, the authors quote H. Raup, who, they say, "cautioned against the romantic glorification of 'wilder is better.'"

I guess that makes me a romantic. I do believe that wilder is better, at least in some places. I believe that we should manage some of our wild lands just for wildlife, not for people. I believe that even when we manage wild places for people, we can and should

find ways to accommodate the needs of wild things. I believe that
sometimes we should put the needs of wildlife above our own. I
do believe that wild things have a right to existence. I believe these
things passionately, spiritually, idealistically, romantically.

Scientists often dismiss romantics, we poor, deluded Don Quixotes,
who can't see reality for the windmill arms. We romantics are emotional, messy, illogical, and, well, unscientific. Scientists seek to
understand all the rules that govern nature. Nothing pleases a scientist more than to discover some sort of first principle that defines the
way the world works.

Underlying the scientist's search for knowledge is a desire to
make life better. The idea is, once science has winkled out all the
rules of the universe, once we understand how everything works,
then we'll be able to bend nature to our will. We'll be able to use
nature to accomplish whatever we want. We'll vanquish disease,
banish hunger, access unlimited energy, live forever in harmony. It's
a kind of back-to-Eden vision, only with a lot more instrumentation.
So who's the romantic now?

The dictionary defines the Romantic Movement, which began in
the late eighteenth century, as a movement characterized by "freedom of form and spirit." To me, freedom of form and spirit *is* the
wild. More important, it is the meaning of wild, a place that directs
itself without human interference, without the order that we humans
seek to impose on all of creation.

While I was watching the ducks and shorebirds going about their
business, one of the geese raised its head suddenly. It listened a
moment and then began honking in alarm. The shorebirds froze in
place. Their brown, black, and white feathers blended in so perfectly
with the mud and water that they seemed to disappear before my
eyes. I knew they were there, but I couldn't see them. In the distance,
I heard several more geese honking overhead. Soon a little flock of
Canada Geese showed up and circled the goose who was calling to
them. After making sure that all was well, they splashed down near
their fellow, and greeting honks were exchanged all around. The
Lagoon residents heaved a collective sigh of relief—ah, false alarm,

no raptors in sight, nothing to worry about. The Lagoon slowly came back to life.

Wild, you see, doesn't mean the same as chaotic or disorganized. The wildlife on the Lagoon is highly organized in the sense that it is woven into an interdependent ecosystem. The shorebirds depend on the geese to give them warning of possible danger. The ducks watch the shorebirds for similar alerts. It's all in balance, one thing depending on another.

Left to itself, the wild stays in this balance. Overpopulation of birds is prevented by the size of the food source and the presence of predators. Without such checks on population, those shorebirds would turn into fat tussock-potatoes, sprawled out in front of a cattail screen with a cool worm on their bellies, letting out the occasional belch. They would multiply beyond the carrying capacity of the land and crowd out other species.

In fact, the Canada Geese at the Fill threaten to do just that. Prior to 1900, Seattle's Canada Geese were migratory. But as hunting decreased and tasty lawns increased, a breeding population of one introduced subspecies, *Branta canadensis moffitti,* became established in the city. These nonnative geese are now fully urbanized birds without sufficient natural controls on their population. From time to time, humans capture and kill them or destroy their eggs, but the geese are such successful breeders that eventually the population rebounds, and they become pests again.

The Fill thus teaches us that it is not the wild that is untrammeled, at least not for long; it is our own unrestricted growth and our meddling that upset the balance of nature. Such lessons are for me one of the best reasons we should preserve natural areas such as the Fill. They teach us restraint and humility.

These are lessons not espoused by the authors of the *Science* article, however. On the contrary, they conclude by wishing for a new science that focuses on tradeoffs rather than impacts when we make ecological decisions. They say that when we can weigh tradeoffs scientifically, we can make the best decision for stewarding nature in perpetuity for people.

Given the spread of our species and our impact on the planet, I suppose that the authors are correct about the need to have some kind of paradigm for making stewardship decisions. And since we're the ones setting up the paradigm, we will undoubtedly set it up with ourselves in mind. But let us then put into the equation a very human value, and let us set that value as among the highest: the human love of wild nature. Edward O. Wilson called this yearning for nature "biophilia," the love of living things. He said it was a basic human need.

I think we all need to see Baird's Sandpipers dipping their bills elegantly to eat insects on an island of mud in the middle of a lagoon in a little patch of wild paradise like the Fill. More than that, I think we all need that whiff of the far north that they bring, for they are a kind of messenger from a vast, unknown wilderness. They tell us that such faraway places still exist, free of civilized humanity and the hubris that makes us believe we matter most. We don't. We are small compared to nature, and we will never fully control the wild.

I may not get to those far-off wild places bodily. I may never see with my own eyes the tundra where the Baird's Sandpipers make their nests, or the endless forests of the north where the chickadees forage. But as long as those places exist in their free and wild state, I can go there every day in my imagination. As I do.

21. What's Your Evidence?

Scientific genealogy is all the rage right now. People by the thousands are scrubbing their inner cheeks with swabs and sending their DNA samples to commercial testing companies in hopes that they will discover royalty, or at least a little nobility, among their ancestors. Not me. I'm proud to say that I'm one of what Leona Helmsley called the little people. Serfs, peasants, maids, the help—that's where I come from. My family undoubtedly spent more time washing the royal coach than riding in it.

As a certified member of what you might call the oblige half of the noblesse equation, I have never moved a mountain, never parted a sea. I've been a secretary, a dental assistant, an editor, a teacher. All worthy occupations, all helping make the world a better place, but not the stuff of legends. I know I'm never going to get the accolades or the attention that the glitterati so routinely receive. In secret, I may practice my Queen Elizabeth wave against the day that some civic group might ask me to appear on a parade float. But then reality intrudes, and I know that I'm unlikely to show up even at the Fremont Summer Solstice Parade, a neighborhood parade where participants exuberantly self-select to march, sometimes in the nude. I'm way too shy, for one thing.

We toilers in the human vineyard seldom see the fruits of our labors. We have to have faith that the little bits of care we give to others do indeed bear fruit, but we rarely get the chance to see this for ourselves. I remember talking to Aki Kurose about this. Aki was a first-grade teacher at Laurelhurst Elementary School. She was beloved by the kids because she respected them. Aki often got the most difficult children assigned to her classroom because she believed in all children and was willing to work with anyone. One year, she got a boy who came from a very bad environment and was deeply disturbed. Whenever he became upset, he would get down on the floor and roll. Sometimes he would roll for most of the day.

Aki worked with that boy diligently. She had never in her life given up on a kid, and she wasn't about to give up on this one. When the year had passed and the kids had all left for summer vacation, I asked Aki how the year had gone. "It was just great," she replied.

"What about the boy who rolled?" I asked. "How did he do?"

"Oh, he was great, too. By the end of the year, he wasn't rolling as much."

I've often thought about that story and what it means. Some people might interpret that story negatively and say, "Well, isn't that just dandy. She taught that kid for a whole year, and look how little she accomplished."

But that's not the meaning of Aki's work at all. Aki knew that boy needed a lot more help than she could give him in just one year. She also knew it would be better for all of us if that boy received the help he needed, because next year he was going to be back at the same school interacting with the same kids. Some day, he was going to be a grown man living in our community. The question was: What kind of a man would he be?

Aki believed that if the adults in that kid's life worked with him and never gave up on him, he had the potential to be a fine, educated person who could give back to the world. She saw in him the potential to be something good and strong. She also accepted the fact that she herself played only a small part in his development and would probably never know what became of him. She had to be satisfied with the little contribution that she had made: by the end of the year, he wasn't rolling as much.

A psychologist friend of mine from Juneau, John Jensen, used to say that people make emotional and intellectual judgments based on what he called an evidence system. What evidence do we have for drawing a particular conclusion, or forming a particular opinion? In Aki's case, the fact that her student wasn't rolling around on the floor all day long was evidence that he had made progress. In her view, forward progress was what education is all about, and so therefore, that kid had had a successful year.

In my own life, I too am faced with intractable problems, as are we all. For me, one of the most pressing problems is the environment. What evidence do I have about how the environment is doing?

Well, there is plenty of evidence of doom: global warming; the growing energy demands of ginormous developing countries such as China, India, and Indonesia; plummeting bird populations. You know the litany.

There is also plenty of evidence for hope: improved air quality in the United States; the return of raptors from the brink of extinction; the success of the Nature Conservancy's strategy combining land purchases with conservation easements to maximize the preservation of important ecosystems.

The problem I have with judging an issue as big as saving the environment, however, is that no amount of evidence can measure the degree of success I myself can achieve. Because I am one of the little people, the things that I can do personally seem too small, and the problem seems too large. The evidence I see around the world—either pro or con—does not give me much traction to get going and do anything to make a difference. My efforts are a drop in the bucket, and sometimes I feel that the bucket can get along just fine without me. Aki would be appalled.

What I need is not evidence, but inspiration. For that, I always go to the Fill.

One day in summer, feeling like the inspiration tank was just about out of gas, I plunked my camp stool down at the edge of the Southwest Pond. I turned my back to the trail and the traffic and focused on the pond before me. It was my feeble attempt to shut out a stressful, too-big world that was making my stomach churn.

The pond itself is not beautiful by conventional standards. Scum covers its surface, and dead snags poke up like petrified strands of

Medusa's hair. But cattails wave in the breeze, too, and wildflowers bloom. In my curmudgeonly mood, I noted that some of those wildflowers are Garden Loosestrife, a plant all too accurately termed noxious by the state. Garden Loosestrife is an invasive plant from Europe, and when it comes to a new place, it takes over if it can. People brought loosestrife to the U.S. because they thought it was a pretty ornamental flower, and then they turned it loose into our unprotected environment.

As my thoughts turned to the dark side again, I heard two birds chipping in the willow beside my head. I froze. Soon a Common Yellowthroat popped into view just inches away. It was a juvenile, newly come into this tired old world of ours. Common Yellowthroats are members of the wood-warbler family who come here in the spring to breed. They stay through the summer and then return to Central and South America in the fall. At the Fill, you can often find them nesting near water.

The bird cocked its head at me, black eye glinting in the sun. It was so close I could see the delicate edges of its feathers lift slightly in the breeze. The yellow of its throat shaded into cream and olive on its breast. Its little feet clutched the reed to which it clung. It stayed like that for a second, perhaps two, and then twitched its tail and hopped onto a branch. It began chipping again, answered by another yellowthroat. Its mother? A sibling? I don't know. I caught only a brief glimpse of the second bird.

Meanwhile the first bird, having decided that I posed no immediate threat, came back to its reed perch. It gave me a short glance, just to make sure I was not going to eat it, then it flicked its way along the foliage, picking up bugs here and there. If it stayed still for more than a second, I could have seen its tiny heart beating, but it never stayed still that long. Hunting, flicking, pecking, crouching, leaping, flapping, chipping—that tiny creature was filled from head to claw with the very force of life itself. Amazing that something so small could be so alive.

Watching that young bird in action, I thought about the day my oldest son went to boot camp to become a U.S. Marine. He had been told that the Marine Corps would provide everything for him, so he walked out the door carrying absolutely nothing. I stopped him and asked where was his bag? He said he didn't need anything. I asked him, "Not even a toothbrush?" Nope, the Marines would provide. But what, I asked, if the Marines were a little slow in providing a toothbrush? Shouldn't he take a backup toothbrush, as a kind of Plan B dental insurance? No. He left unencumbered by anything, as free as a bird.

What does it mean to be free as a bird?

It's a complicated answer. Surely, birds are not burdened by tax forms to fill out, as we are every April. They don't have to worry about what the stock market will do, or whether the wheezy old car will pass the state's emissions test, please, please, please, just one more time. On the other hand, birds cannot be said to have much free will, either. Is that a burden, or is it freedom?

I cannot say. All I know is that soon the Common Yellowthroat I saw will leap into the sky and head south for the winter, driven by urges it cannot understand. It will leave unencumbered by anything, certainly not a toothbrush. It will somehow find its way to its wintering grounds and live there till spring, when it will fly all the way back to the pond near the Dime Lot. It will be less than a year old, and yet it will do this. No human being could achieve the same.

Surely, such a wonderment should be preserved at all costs. Yet what can one little person do? Scientist Dexter Chapin addressed this issue in an interview conducted by three sixth-grade girls, who were writing an oral history book about Seattle Academy. In the course of the interview, the girls asked Chapin why he liked to teach science at Seattle Academy.

This is how he answered: "I've worked at a whole lot of schools. I've been teaching for 35 years. Believe it or not, Seattle Academy is the most feminine school I have ever worked at. Now let me explain what I mean by that. If you go and talk to boys, you find out that when a boy does something wrong, other boys want justice. They want somebody punished. They want him to pay the price. They want the rules supported.

"The girls, on the other hand, when somebody does something wrong, think it rips the social fabric. What girls are really interested in is repairing the social fabric, making the social fabric good again. In this school, when people screw up and rip the social fabric, the school responds by trying to reweave the social fabric, not by necessarily 'punishing' the student but by making the student do things. I mean, it isn't a free ride. But the point is that everything that the school does to the student is about reweaving the social fabric. I like that about this school."

Listening to Chapin explain about the social fabric made a light bulb turn on in my mind. I realized that any hole in the fabric of life, no matter how small, weakens the entire cloth. Therefore, anything that I can do to repair even the smallest hole is significant. It matters.

I may be one of the little people. I cannot, by my own single efforts, end war and keep young Marines safe. I can't stop global warming. I can't restore the vast flyways that supported untold billions of migrating birds. But maybe I can make that ugly little pond by the Dime Lot a little better for the Common Yellowthroat when it returns. Maybe I can pull a few invasive plants, or give a little money to the Center for Urban Horticulture so they can do more to keep the Fill healthy.

I can also show friends and family the wonder of that tiny bird. I can explain how a little warbler made me smile when I thought about how much it had in common with a big, tough, soon-to-be Marine who left behind his old life and took off on a new adventure as free as a bird.

Most of all, I can hope that others will see the Common Yellowthroat as I do and bend every effort to make just a little bit of the world better. If kindness and caring for our planet can multiply, if even one small act by one little person can spread, think what we could do.

Pull a weed, help a child, move a mountain, save a planet.

22. Hope Seen Clearly

August is the month when all the floral chickens come home to roost. The weeds you didn't pull out in April reach epic proportions in August. The grass you didn't cut in May is too high for an ordinary mower now—you've got to get a tractor. The tomato plants you meant to take out of their two-inch pots and replant in your loamy raised beds have withered next to the beds that never got raised, loamily or otherwise.

At the Fill, August is the month when the many species of non-native, invasive plants grow head-high and you can see exactly how big your problems really are: the Himalayan Blackberry bushes that, like zombies, seem impossible to kill; the Queen Anne's Lace that looks so beautiful but shouldn't be here; the Yellow Iris that is doing its best to occupy every wet patch of mud still unbaked by the sun. Of all the threats to the Fill, invasive species pose the biggest. I saw this for myself at the Main Pond, the biggest pond on the site.

When I began birding the Fill back in the 1980s, the Main Pond was shrouded so thickly with native cattails that you could see the water in only a few places. Shorebirds and marsh birds were abundant, if frustrating to try and see. You couldn't possibly approach the pond without a lookout Marsh Wren blaring your presence to all and sundry. Red-winged Blackbird males swooped out to attack your head, urged on by a raucous female audience that would join in the flyby if they thought the males weren't being aggressive enough. Common Yellowthroats would pop up and down to see what the fuss was about, while I would hurry along trying to get to a break in the bushes before all the shorebirds had fled. Anytime the blackbird brigade failed in its duty, the Killdeers would take over. They'd scramble into the air with sirens going full blast. I might as well have been carrying a bullhorn: Warning! All birds leave the area immediately! Connie is coming!

"Don't you guys recognize me?" I'd ask in exasperation. "I've been coming here every single day." Finally one day, I wore a floppy blue hat to keep the hair out of my eyes. Something about that hat convinced the birds that I was okay. Maybe they thought I was another bird, a somewhat overlarge bird with a beak placed rather high on its head, but still one of the in-crowd. Whatever the reason, the marsh birds stayed silent and allowed me to creep in to watch the shorebirds. As I recall, there were banks of shorebirds feeding in stripes along the shore: the Least Sandpipers highest on land among the grasses, the Western Sandpipers just dipping their toes in the water, and the dowitchers up to their bellies in deeper water. It was a primeval cafeteria with seating by sections. I was enchanted.

I can't tell you when the Purple Loosestrife first arrived at the Main Pond. Purple Loosestrife is an invasive plant from Europe. It was introduced to this continent as an ornamental and medicinal flower and got out into the wild. When it shows up in marshy habitat like the Fill, it usually takes over quickly, driving out native species. Washington State has classified Purple Loosestrife as a Class B noxious weed, meaning landowners are required to remove it if feasible or if required by the county.

Purple Loosestrife has been present at the Fill for decades. In fact, Harry Higman and Earl Larrison reported it in their 1951 book, *Union Bay, the Life of a City Marsh.* But it had somehow been contained in small areas prior to the 1990s. Something changed then, and the loosestrife began to invade all the ponds aggressively, driving out the native plants.

I didn't notice its arrival at the Main Pond at first. Gradually as the loosestrife moved in, the cattails went away, but the encroaching loosestrife seemed like a natural succession to me, clueless as I was about invasive species. Then one day, I encountered Scotsman and master birder Stuart MacKay, who berated me about allowing loosestrife to take over our pond. "You Americans don't realize what you have here," I remember he said. "You take it all for granted, but you're losing it."

In typical Scots fashion, Stuart showed up the next weekend and, without permission from anyone, began chopping and pulling out the loosestrife. "Is that allowed?" I wondered to myself. Then, "I don't care," I answered and joined him to pull.

That summer, we did everything we could to encourage others to help us pull out the loosestrife. At one point, we had something like 20 volunteers in the work parties, all heaving on loosestrife that had grown to be more than six feet tall, with roots holding onto mud balls so large that I couldn't lift one by myself. We told everyone we knew to tell everyone they knew to come and pull. Boy Scouts came to clear out the loosestrife in the cottonwood pond north of East Point. A church group came to rid the Southeast Pond of all the loosestrife. It took them three or four weekends, but they showed up religiously. Students who owed community service to their schools got permission to perform their service at the Fill, pulling out loosestrife. I remember one boy who was terrified of bees, but he squared his shoulders and pulled up flowering loosestrife with dozens of bees on each stalk.

By the time the fall migration started, we had cleared out all the loosestrife around the Main Pond, Shoveler's Pond, the cottonwood pond, and the Southeast Pond. On one of the last days of our work party, I was at the south end of the Main Pond, pulling at a plant that was stubbornly hanging onto its root ball out in the water when three dowitchers flew in and landed almost at my feet. As soon as they hit the water, all three heads dived deep and began moving rapidly up and down, stitching for food.

All of us stopped pulling and watched these lovely wild creatures fattening up for their flight south. We could imagine them coming in from the north, tired and hungry from a journey that was already arduous, and yet they had farther to go. We could think back to a time when all of Puget Sound would have been laid out with dinner

for them, but now the Fill was one of the few places left in the Puget Sound Trough where these birds could stop, rest, feed, and prepare to fly on. Because of our efforts, the dowitchers had a rich habitat loaded with life-giving critters for them to eat. Watching them go at it was the best and only thank-you we needed. Tired, dirty, and stinking from the mud that was so plentifully endowed with goose poop, we smiled at each other in perfect happiness.

The next spring, I had high hopes that we would be able to attack the loosestrife that choked the Dime Lot pond and the ponds along the road leading in. Alas, many of our work party members failed to show up. The call went out, but few answered. Stuart and my husband did the work of 20, but often they and I were the only ones pulling that year. I can't explain it. Maybe people felt that they had been there, done that, job over. Maybe they couldn't face the backbreaking labor and the bees. Maybe their own lives had consumed their energy, leaving them with nothing to give back to nature. Maybe they had lost hope.

We did our best that year, but we managed to keep only the Main Pond and Shoveler's Pond clear. After that, every year was a harder struggle. Sometimes, students from the UW's Restoration Ecology Network would clear out loosestrife, but there was always plenty that grew back. At one point, Stuart bought a gas-powered weed whacker and tried to keep the flowers from making more seeds, but the loosestrife was clearly winning. Then one day, I saw large loosestrife plants growing out in the cattails deep in the marsh bordering Union Bay. I knew then that our fight was nearing its end. There was no way we could pull out loosestrife in areas that we couldn't reach. I told Stuart the news. He just looked at me and then went back to weeding. I did the same, but my heart wasn't in it.

I confess there were days when the mere thought of going to the Fill was painful. I felt guilty that somehow I had personally failed. I believed there must exist a key somewhere that would unlock people's hearts and muscles and get them to come in vast numbers to pull out every last one of those vile plants that were killing my beloved Fill. But I couldn't find the key. I didn't have the right words that would motivate people to volunteer, and yet I call myself a writer.

At my lowest point and dreading another fruitless year of pulling, I paid a visit one spring to meet my nemesis and find out what kind of a battle it was going to be. Instead of vigorous young plants, I found withered stalks covered with brown leaves. The leaves had holes in them. As I walked among the dying plants, I looked down and saw dozens of bugs on my legs. My initial reaction was to let out a high-pitched "Ewwww!" and start dancing around, shaking my pants legs like I had just become the favorite entry in the St. Vitus Day Dance-a-thon.

I found out later that the insects were *Galerucella* beetles from Europe. They were here to war with the wicked. After much study, botanists had decided the best way to fight loosestrife was with biological controls. Expectations were that the beetles would eventually control 90 percent of the Purple Loosestrife.

The plan worked. The beetles did a real number on the loosestrife that first year, attacking the leaves vigorously. In the second year, after successfully overwintering in the fields, the bugs did even better. I think that year, not a single loosestrife plant around the Main Pond flowered.

It's been many years now since anyone has had to pull Purple Loosestrife by hand. The birds have not rebounded as we had hoped they would, and the cattails have not come back, but the mud is there, waiting. I am confident that any shorebird who decides to stop off for a while will find rich pickings, enough to refuel for the migration flight ahead.

I talked to one of the botantists shortly after the bugs had proven their worth. I told him I was a member of the loosestrife-pulling crew that had struggled for so many years to clear the ponds. "Well, you see your efforts were useless," he said. "While you were doing that, we were studying the safety of releasing insects from Europe. We wanted to make sure that we weren't going to be introducing a bigger problem if we released them here. When we were certain that the insects were safe, we released them, and now look at the results.

If you had just waited, those results would have been the same." He turned and left me standing there, speechless.

"Hmph," I finally muttered, not knowing what else to say. Then I went home and re-read my favorite play, *Cyrano de Bergerac*. In the last scene, Cyrano is felled by a log dropped on his head by his enemies. He realizes that he will not die gloriously in battle—as he had always dreamed—but ignominiously in obscurity. Nevertheless, he struggles to his feet and cries: "Let the old fellow come now! He shall find me on my feet, sword in hand. I can see him there. He grins...What's that you say? Hopeless? Why, very well. But a man does not fight merely to win...You there, who are you? A hundred against one. I know them now, my ancient enemies—falsehood! There! There! Prejudice, compromise, cowardice. What's that you say? Surrender? No! Never, never! I fight on. I fight on. I fight on."

There are round circles that dot the page where Cyrano says his last speech. They are my tearstains. I weep not from despair but from the sheer emotional bond I share with all of humanity when we choose hope in the face of almost certain defeat. We cannot be defeated in any struggle if we refuse to give up our hope and belief in the things that make us most noble as humans: kindness, courage, generosity, and love, not just for each other but for the Earth itself.

What that botanist told me was a harsh truth told brutally, but was it the only truth?

I say there was a deeper truth in what we did. I say that we kept the Fill alive for shorebirds until a more permanent solution was found, and I say that we did so by our own effort. I say that we built a community, however imperfect, who worked together to save something well worth saving. I say that people who love the environment should take heart and never give up. You may encounter setbacks in your struggle, but you can never be defeated if you just keep getting up.

As Dr. Jerome Groopman said in an interview I heard on National Public Radio in February 2004, "Many of us confuse hope with optimism, a prevailing attitude that 'things turn out for the best.' But hope differs from optimism. Hope does not arise from being told to 'think positively,' or from hearing an overly rosy forecast. Hope, unlike optimism, is rooted in unalloyed reality... Hope is the elevating feeling we experience when we see—in the mind's eye—a path to a better future. Hope acknowledges the significant obstacles and deep pitfalls along that path. True hope has no room for delusion."

In other words, hope is not a Pollyannish naïveté. It is a consciously chosen way of life. Living with hope means we commit ourselves to search for a path forward—no matter how big the challenge that faces us—because we know we can be better, do better, make the world better.

The history of human progress is the history of hope.

23. We're in This Together

Pete Dunne, that famous birding author, often comments that birders are the nicest people he knows. "The ethic of sharing," he writes, "runs strong among birders because birds are things that can be shared." When I read that, I can't help but think of one of my earliest birding experiences.

My family and I had driven out to the coast to see what we could see. My notes from that era indicate that we could have seen 243 species on our road trip. We saw 45. We actually saw more birds, of course, but who knew what they were? Even then, I was in love with this simultaneously frustrating and exhilarating activity called birding. I never knew what I would find around the next bend in the road, and if I did find something, I couldn't predict whether I would be able to identify it. Birding, for me, is a high-order-of-magnitude treasure hunt.

In Westport, the best bird we found was a Great Egret foraging in the fields of the airport. What a stately, angelic bird. We watched it until our two little boys threatened to implode, then we got back in the van and drove over to Tokeland.

Far out on a spit of brackish marsh, we saw two birders with expensive scopes intently watching something in the distance. Still high on our Great Egret, we piled out of our van like a litter of puppies and rolled over to the birders to ask what they were scoping. The birders took one look at our crummy little scope on its pathetic tripod, our two kids wearing cheap binoculars, the one pair of battered binoculars that my husband and I shared, and our beaming faces.

They must have decided we were rank amateurs—bird"watchers" rather than bird"ers"—because they didn't answer. Thinking they were hard of hearing, my husband asked them more loudly what they were seeing. In supercilious tones, one finally replied, "It's the godwit flock." Implicit in his tone was the addendum, "you idiot."

All the sunbeams went out of my boys' faces. I felt my temper rise. In my family, the only one who gets to call my husband an idiot—even implicitly—is me. Enunciating as clearly as I could, I said to John, "Oh, the godwit flock. I guess you can set up the scope for that, but I'd rather see something more exotic, like that Great Egret we just found."

The two birders straightened up and exchanged a look. "Where did you see a Great Egret?" one finally asked.

When I told them Westport, there was a faint popping sound, like a paper airplane that had just hit Mach 1, and they were gone.

John said, "Do you think that Great Egret will still be there when they arrive?"

"I certainly hope not," I replied.

John was shocked. He lectured me about kindness, about returning good for ill, about turning the other cheek. John is a Methodist by upbringing, whose father taught Sunday school for decades, so he knows all the biblical strictures against sin. He trotted them out until I had to admit that I had done wrong by wishing those birders bad luck. But while I was good on the outside, I was bad on the inside. I still hoped the birders would miss the egret when they got to Westport. They had been mean for no reason and had made my kids sad.

This incident came to mind yesterday when I was out at the Fill. Bob Schultz, birder extraordinaire of Totem Lake, tracked me down at Shoveler's Pond. He said he'd been carrying around a book for the past few days in hopes of finding me so he could give it to me. We talked for an hour about birds, politics, nature, and life. As Bob left, videographer Al Wagar appeared with his videocam. He offered to take me into the CUH library to show me his latest DVD about birds of Washington State. Gardener Doug Schmitt wanted to talk about perches and nest boxes for Violet-green and Tree Swallows. Photographer Katie Lloyd had a CD she had burned so she could give me her latest photos. Birder Evan Houston stopped for a moment to catch me up on the latest birds he'd seen at the Fill, and when a couple of non-birders wanted to know what we were looking at, he very kindly spent time telling them. When I finally got in my car to return home, I recalled Pete Dunne's saying: Birders really are the nicest people I know.

I also recalled something my father told me once. He and a bunch of his friends from work had retired to Lake Havasu City in Arizona. There, they had formed a little community of retirees who spent their golden years having fun together. They took bus rides to Nevada to gamble. They played card games at night. They gave dinner parties for each other.

One member of the community drove everyone else more or less crazy. "Eddie" was foul-mouthed and cheap. He never paid his fair share. He cheated at cards when he thought he could get away with it, and he would never admit that he lost any money at the casinos. Eddie always won, according to him. This last trait was especially irritating to my dad, who lost all too frequently. One day, my dad was recounting the latest Eddie escapade and concluded by saying, "Well, Eddie is just like that." Everybody in the group nodded. Yep, Eddie was just like that.

It made me realize that my dad and his friends knew things about community that are important for me and my Me Generation to learn. Community is a precious thing. It gives you the chance to share your experiences—your happiness as well as your troubles. It holds you up when you need help. It strengthens each person and multiplies everyone's contributions.

Communities are not perfect. They're hard to build and easy to destroy. To build one up, you have to give something of yourself, which takes time and effort. You also have to remember that you don't necessarily get to choose everyone who belongs in your community. Some in the community are going to be pains, but they are just as much members as everyone else is—and maybe sometimes

you're a pain, too. We all have our foibles, and we aren't always going to agree on everything. But we all do agree on the most important thing: that we are in this together.

The birding community in our state is made up of hundreds of different people with hundreds of different ideas about birding. Some people are in it because they care about the environment and use birding as a reason to advocate for better stewardship. Some people are in it because their spouses or friends roped them in. Some like to list. Some like to band. Some think raptors are the only birds worth caring about. Some think the same about shorebirds. Some devote every spare moment to birding. Some put out a feeder in their backyard and just like to enjoy whatever dicky-bird appears.

The wonderful thing about birding is that it provides such a big tent. There is something in it for everyone. Best of all, there's no right way or wrong way to care about birds.

We need to remember this, not only because having a community that cares about each other is more fun, more exciting, more educational, and more productive. We need to keep our big tent big because there simply are not enough of us to save the world by ourselves: not enough listers, not enough citizen-scientists, not enough banders, not enough backyard bird feeders, not enough poets, not enough ecobusinesses.

I read the other day that in the year 2000, there were an estimated 69 million people in North America who watched birds in some fashion. That sounds like a lot until you realize that it is only about 22 percent of our population. In other words, 78 percent of us in North America don't watch birds, don't care about them, would rather do other things with our limited resources. Let's face it: birders are down on the narrow end of the bell curve. Furthermore, the U.S. Census Bureau estimates that by the year 2020, there will be 7.7 billion people on Earth. Sixty-nine million birdwatchers in North America is less than one percent of the world's population.

Unless we can figure out ways to get more people interested in the birds we love, we will find ourselves isolated and unheard. It won't matter that our love of birds is also a love for the natural world, and that it is absolutely crucial for the natural world to stay healthy. People will put their own short-term interests first, and all our doomsaying will get us nowhere. Remember Cassandra?

We need every member of our community, and more. Listers need the poets. Scientists need the hobbyists. Banders need the backyarders. Serious birders need the casual folks who want us to tell them what that funny red bird was that came to their yard one day last year, cocked an eye at the lawn, reached down, and then pulled out a fat, juicy worm. We need the biggest community that we can possibly build.

As for those curmudgeons of long ago, I confess I am still trying to figure out how curmudgeonliness fits into our community. I'm sure there's a place somewhere for surly birders. Maybe they're the ones who can scold the dog-walkers who let their dogs run free over nesting habitat at the Fill, or perhaps they can glare at the bikers who decide it would be fun to start creating their own dirt-bike track on the prairie so painstakingly hand-planted with native grasses.

Wait a minute. Isn't that what I do? Wasn't there that time I yelled at the photographers who were off-trail trying to photograph a rare bird? Didn't I lecture the little boys who were skipping stones across the Main Pond while a mother Gadwall and nine chicks were floating nearby? And what about the glare I gave the guy who jogs with his dog off-leash, a glare so gimlet-eyed that now he turns around and runs the other way whenever he sees me?

Could I have more in common with those Great Egret chasers than I thought? Could I possibly be a—gasp!—curmudgeon myself??

Nah, humbug.

24. One Hot Day

August is normally one of my favorite months because the early signs of fall are everywhere, and I love the fall. By August, the shorebird migration is in full swing, as the adults leave their babies behind on the breeding grounds and head south for the winter. It's not a case of parental abandonment. Shorebird babies are born precocial, meaning they are able to take care of themselves very soon after hatching, so they don't need their parents to feed them or keep them warm or guard them against predators. However, the babies are unable to fly at first, so they have to stay behind on the breeding grounds to grow their flight feathers and build up their strength. By late August or early September, they too will begin to come through the Fill on their first journey.

It's fun to see these youngsters—mind you, only a few weeks old—having such a big adventure. Now that my own kids are all in their twenties, I have become very interested in how other species manage to launch their young. Shorebird launchings are among nature's most enviable.

Another reason I like August is that there is a crispness to the dawn air. In the mornings, the slanting sunbeams light up the leaves that are just beginning to turn to soft gold, and the heavy heads of the fescue grass cast little shadows on the trail. Yes, fall is a beautiful season at the Fill.

But not today. Summer fought back tenaciously today, refusing to retreat to the southern hemisphere where it belongs. A high pressure zone squatted over Western Washington, ushering in hot, muggy air from Oregon.

Now, I don't want to sound prejudiced here, and I have no intention of offending the sun lovers amongst us, but I despise the summer. It's too sunny, for one thing. Where are my beloved Seattle-gray clouds? It's also too dry. And much too hot. My brain has a melting point of 80 degrees. Today, predictions were for temperatures in the 90s.

I got to the Fill early, in hopes that I could beat the heat. No such luck. The sun was already hammering down in full fury, making the flora and me droop with fatigue. The air was so still, not even the cottonwood leaves were wiggling. Beads of sweat rolled down my face as I trudged along the grass path bordering the Main Pond.

I'm very Victorian in my beliefs about sweat. I don't think we should do it. My Iowan husband tells me that sweat is nature's air conditioner, designed to cool us as the moisture on our skin evaporates. Evidently the air conditioner was on the fritz this day because the relative humidity was too high. I dragged my sorry self to the south end of the pond, unfolded my camp stool, and flopped. It was so hot that both the birds and I could only sit panting with our beaks open.

Not a thing was stirring. Everyone who could find refuge had done so. A Great Blue Heron stood in the water under the willows, cooling its feet. Even the swallows, normally in the air from sunup to sundown, had settled into the bushes. You don't fly a marathon, or anything else, in such conditions—heat prostration would kill you.

As my cortex began to melt, pooling into a puddle down near my brainstem, one feeble thought occurred: *must find shade.* I hauled myself up and headed for the cottonwoods at East Point. There were no birds there whatsoever, but by this time I didn't care. There was plenty of shade, and that was what mattered.

Slowly, the coolness of the glade revived me, and I began to appreciate the beauty that is the Fill. The lake lay quiet before me, mirror-smooth. To the west, vast tracts of water lilies were separated by runways of clear water, like a liquid tarmac beckoning the birds to come in for a safe landing. A vee of Canada Geese came skimming over the surface, doubling themselves with their reflections.

Claude Monet, that artist of lilies and light, would have been just as enchanted as I was.

When the geese flew over the shore, they flushed a Green Heron, who exploded out of the cattails and then landed on a tiny island of mud just a few feet away from where I sat. The heron saw me and debated. Usually, Green Herons are shy creatures who dislike attention. If they see people watching them, they leave. This one began muttering under its breath, like a chicken about to lay an egg. I froze into a statue, afraid even to breathe. To my left, a Virginia Rail started clicking, and a Marsh Wren in the cattails began to scold. The other birds' sounds seemed to reassure the heron, who settled down to hunt for fish.

The heron's fishing hole was exceptionally productive on this day. I timed the bird's catches. It was taking one minnow every three minutes, on average. With its feet firmly fixed in the mud, it would slowly unwind a few inches of neck, sight a fish, aim, and stab. Back would come its bill, laden with a fish. A quick swallow, and then it returned to the hunt.

Fish were not its only prey. When a large, blue dragonfly flew too close, the heron grabbed it right out of the air, juggled it into head-first position, and then gulped. The dragonfly's wings got stuck briefly, then with a crackle disappeared down the hatch.

In between courses, the heron would preen. At one point, it unfolded one wing like an umbrella and stuck its head underneath, upside down. It looked like a teenage boy on a date, checking out his armpits to make sure he was socially acceptable. I couldn't help but laugh, which reminded the heron of my presence. It clucked some more, wondering whether to go or stay. Luckily, the fishing hole was evidently so productive that the heron decided to put up with me. I was the one who finally left. A few clouds had drifted overhead, and the heat wasn't so bad. Besides, I was so elevated by the heron's grace in admitting me into its world, what did a little heat matter? It was a beautiful summer day. I beamed.

One of the many charms of birding is that it puts you into the moment, and by doing so, it eliminates the passage of time. There is no past, no future. There *is* a steady progression from one moment to the next, but each point on the timeline is complete unto itself, holding on to its perfection before giving way to the next perfect moment. No clock marks these transitions. Most of all, there is no schedule to keep.

We take for granted our subjugation to schedules. In our culture, especially nowadays, schedules rule our lives. We make appointments. We keep a social calendar. We have to-do lists with deadlines. In order to keep to a schedule, we need to know what time it is at all points along the day. Punctuality is a virtue, lateness a vice. To make sure that I am never late, I have seven clocks in my house and four wristwatches, as well as numerous digital devices that also keep time. Our five computers, the oven, my cell phone, and even my coffeemaker can all tell me what time it is. It's not just that they can; they do, adding a kind of compulsion to my life that forces me to be aware of what time it is during every waking moment.

In our society, we submit even further to the tyranny of time. Because we can keep track of every moment, we seem to feel it is necessary to fill each one of them with some kind of productive activity. Lawyers call this billable hours, and they are not alone. My plumber keeps track of billable half-hours. Heaven forbid that he or any of the rest of us wastes even a nanosecond. This is the first day of the rest of your life, you know. Tempus fugit. The moving finger writes, and having writ, moves on. Time is money, life is short, and procrastination is the thief of time.

There is another reason why we'd better make wise use of our time: lately there seems to be a lot less of it. Like Alice, we have to run as hard as we can just to keep in the same place. If we want to get somewhere else, we must run at least twice as fast.

As the pace of our lives keeps accelerating, our slavery to the almighty schedule tightens. No one has any free time anymore; we have leisure time, a very different thing. Leisure time means we have to *productively* relax so that we can quickly return to the servitude of our busy schedule, refreshed and able to increase our productivity even more.

Is there any upper limit on how productive we can be? No. Like perfection, we may never attain ultimate productivity, but we should always aspire to reach it. We may have done a great job today, but tomorrow we can do even better, so we'd better get cracking. Thus we create for ourselves the perfect guilt machine.

I suppose one of the most magical things about the Fill is that somehow, when I enter its borders, I shed all the guilt about stealing a moment out of time. Because nature follows a cyclical pattern, not a linear one, when I am in nature, it never feels as though time is moving forward. Rather, time is a circle that comes back each year to the same place, just as the Earth orbits the sun round and round.

Cosmologists may tell us that our solar system is actually rocketing forward through space, and we are not on an endless merry-go-round. Our galaxy is moving ahead briskly, too. They both have a vector, a direction that starts out at one point and goes to the next at a measurable speed. As in space, so in time: our universe, like our puny lives, travels from this moment to that. The universe had a beginning, the Big Bang, and will inevitably have an end. It's expanding at the moment, but eventually the red shift will turn to blue, and we'll be well on our way to oblivion.

But this is not real for us. We are too small to notice these cosmic movements, too short-lived to absorb the lifespan of the stars. What is real is the ticking of the clock, the sweep of the second hand or the inexorable LED display that shows the big red one turning into a two, the two becoming a three, the three a four, and now we're running late.

Time, for us, is thus largely a cultural invention, but nature is not. Nature is creation itself—timeless and eternal.

When I share the morning with a Green Heron on a hot day in August, neither one of us has a deadline to meet or a schedule to keep. The heron cannot waste time because it knows not what time is. I do know, but when I get lost in the moment of the heron's world, I can forget time itself. And I am free.

Part IV
Fall

25. The Least Sign of Fall

Birders know that the Julian calendar is all wrong. For one thing, the four seasons are definitely not divided into four equal parts, nor do they change on the solstices and equinoxes. The seasons are really more like a map I've seen that illustrates how New Yorkers think of U.S. geography. New York is shown filling up a good half of the map, while Seattle appears as a tiny needle—the Space Needle, to be precise—stuck on the extreme northwest edge of the continent.

Like that map, we here in Seattle could draw a similar chart of the four seasons, showing some huge and others teeny. Winter, for example, is pretty short. It begins in December, when the clouds sock in. Seattleites can go for weeks without seeing the sun. Even when the sun does show up, it seems to believe it had better restrict itself to a limited number of hours. Daytime starts at 7:30 a.m. and wraps up by 4:00 p.m. Working people in windowless cubicles never see daylight at all. For them, the day begins and ends in darkness.

Luckily, winter ends in mid-February, when the first crocuses pop out of the lawn, assuming that the squirrels haven't eaten the crocus bulbs first. If they have, then winter is going to last another six weeks.

Spring begins in March and tapers off in late May, most years. I'm afraid we don't have a name for the last two weeks of February, the period between the end of winter and the beginning of spring. We might have to invent a fifth season for this. My Iowa-born husband says in his home state, they would probably call it Mud.

Summer is by far the shortest of our seasons. Contrary to what hot dog and suntan lotion manufacturers would have you believe,

146

summer begins in June and ends in June. In rainy years, it lasts exactly one day. If you take an overnight trip out of town, you might miss it altogether.

The reason I say summer is so short is because fall is so long. It began today, July 2, and will end in November. How do I know that fall begins so early here? Because today, three adult Least Sandpipers showed up at the Fill on their fall migration to parts south. Least Sandpipers are among the smallest sandpipers in the world, measuring only six inches from beak to tail. They migrate through our state in both spring and fall. I found them this morning as they were busily picking up insects and crustaceans from the mud of the Main Pond. They had stopped briefly to fuel up on their way south.

What a thrill it was to see these drab little creatures in their worn plumage, knowing that they had just come down from the tundra after having completed their parenting duties. Least Sandpipers, like many other members of the shorebird family, aren't saddled with the world's greatest parental responsibilities. Their babies hatch out of the eggs almost completely ready to take care of themselves. A day after the blessed event, the babies leave the nest and start feeding on their own. Shortly after that, the adults leave the breeding grounds and return home. Their young will follow in a couple of months. Home for the Least Sandpipers is a big swath of shore and inland waterway stretching from southern California to South America.

One of the great things about birding is that when you know a bird's natural history, you don't just see the bird in the moment of observation. Rather, you can visualize it surrounded by the experiences it has lived through in the past and that it will continue to have in the future.

Watching the Least Sandpipers here today, I can half-close my eyes and "see" them up on the tundra in May, the males calling attention to themselves and the females sizing up potential mates. I can see the eggs they lay in the short vegetation of the far north. I watch the parents' attempts to camouflage themselves from predators as they brood the eggs, crouching down low on the nest and freezing into immobility whenever a falcon flies overhead. I smile at the babies hatching out, all legs and fluff, everyone feeding happily on the trillions of biting fly and mosquito larvae that would prefer to wait for me and my blood to show up in the flesh, as it were. The flies and mosquitoes wait in vain, for I am not coming this year. I have never come. Someday I will, perhaps. It is my dream.

The Least Sandpipers at the Fill will not stay here long—they have too much farther yet to go. So as I watch them, I can also see the Leasts leaving the Fill, choosing a night when the wind blows softly from the north to help them on their way. I don't think it will be tonight—the birds looked pretty happy with the smorgasbord they were finding on the pond's edge, and I suspect that the Cinnamon Teal sleeping unconcernedly nearby made them feel safe.

I don't know where the Leasts' next stopover will be, exactly—someplace similar to the Fill in Oregon perhaps, or Northern California. I'm also not sure where exactly they will end their journey. These may be Southern California birds, but they might also fly all the way to South America. Some will not make it to their wintering grounds—the falcons know the Leasts' habits very well, after all, and predators are always on the lookout for birds who are too old or too sick or too unwary.

When I look at birds in this expanded way, I am not limited in space, neither am I limited in time. I can look backwards and forwards for as long as Leasts have been Leasts. I can see these birds following the retreat of the glaciers at the end of the Ice Age 12,000 years ago, every year flying a bit farther north to find the tundra and the mosquitoes. I know in years to come they will keep passing through the Fill in spring and fall for as long as we humans can safeguard this sanctuary.

Someone once said, "You can't love what you don't see." I hope everyone will take a moment to look at these little guys from the far north because I know we will keep the Fill safe as long as enough people can see a little piece of history and a little scrap of beauty in three Least Sandpipers heralding the arrival of fall.

26. What's the Point?

We are living through nature's great dance of life now, as birds from the north return home to the Fill from their breeding grounds, and the birds who bred here over the summer start thinking about packing up and heading south. Each species has its own rhythm. They join together at this season, but briefly. Like a minuet in air, the populations bow, circle each other, separate, and move on.

Today at the Fill, all was busy with birdy to-ing and fro-ing. The Red-winged Blackbirds were again present, a new batch from Canada, I think. Red-winged Blackbirds are partial migrants, meaning that some birds migrate, but others stay put. Most of our local blackbirds have been gone for at least a week; only a few remain to dispute a prime cattail or two with the newcomers from the north.

The Tree Swallows and Violet-greens who bred here have already fled. A few Cliff Swallows hang on, but not for long. The Barn Swallows linger the longest of all the swallows, like summer vacationers who make excuses to stay just one more day. Reality will hit, though, in the form of a cold front too brisk for the bugs that presently fill the air and the swallows' bellies. The Barn Swallows will get the message, and one day they, too, will be gone. The skies will feel empty without them.

A House Wren was hopping among the branches around the Southwest Pond. It is only the third House Wren I've ever seen at the Fill. Like the two other House Wrens I've encountered here over the years, this bird was just passing through. It had time enough only to grab a few bites of bugs, and then it had to be on its way.

Three trees farther down the path, two Anna's Hummingbirds got into an argument about a favored perch, as though there were no other perches available in the vast acreage of foliage that the Center for Urban Horticulture folks have been planting this past year. Hummingbirds look like petite, elfin creatures that the merest puff of wind would blow away, but really they are junkyard dogs willing to take on any comers. Argumentative. Volcanic. Bullies, when you come right down to it. I've seen them attack eagles. Football teams would do well to adopt the hummingbird as a mascot—they are much fiercer fighters than huskies, cougars, or even ducks. Any team with a hummingbird for a mascot would be bound to beat the living daylights out of opponents foolish enough to take them on. "We're the mighty HUMMINGBIRDS. Yeah, we're talking to YOU, bub. Grrrr."

In the early morning mist, with the pink sunlight slanting through the trees, I heard a chittering noise above my head. I looked up to see one Vaux's Swift thrashing its wings as fast as it could go, hunting the recent hatch of insects that rose in columns from the damp grass. I wondered where its fellow swifts had gone. Was this one a straggler from the summer flock, or a harbinger of a flock from farther north? No way to tell.

I wandered over to the Main Pond and found a great bird, a Semipalmated Sandpiper, picking at food near the lone Killdeer that has been on guard there all summer. Semipalmated Sandpipers are eastern birds that wander very seldom to the Fill. This one was dressed in spanking white and gray-brown feathers. It looked the picture of health, with its gleaming black bill bluntly picking along the surface of the mud. Did it know it was lost, had flown far off course? What will happen to this sandpiper? Will it keep going south, overwinter in California and return to its correct breeding ground in the spring? Or will it get ever more lost until it dwindles to nothing?

As I gazed at this one bird all alone, I found myself asking, "What is the point?" Sandpipers travel so very far to reach the Arctic to breed in the spring. Imagine the effort they expend. They feed and feed at home in South America during the winter until their breasts become loaded with fat, and then they fly. If they are lucky, they find more food along the way. If not, they feed on their own fat, which melts away till no fat is left and only muscle remains. In a bad year, they feed on their muscles, too.

When they reach their breeding grounds on the tundra in late spring, they mate quickly and have their babies. By late July or early August, the parents are ready to return south, leaving the babies to fend for themselves.

It is thought that the Semipalmated Sandpipers that breed on the eastern tundra in Canada undertake nonstop flights directly over the ocean, flying more than 2,000 miles in one go. Many adults fall along the way, the victims of predators or a hundred other things that might go wrong. The babies embark on the same journey a few weeks later. Somehow, instinct tells the babies the route, a flyway they must traverse without any adult to guide them. The gauntlet awaits them, just as it did their parents.

Sandpipers live such short lives—the shorebirds that I see at the Fill live an average of less than ten years. Some species have a lifespan of less than five years. Each year of their lives, these birds risk everything on the way up north and on the way back. To what end? What is the point of it all?

A naturalist might answer this question by saying, "The point is life itself. Life alone is its own end."

But that's nearly the same as saying, "There is no point."

I unfolded my camp stool and sat to ponder this mystery. Fall melancholia stole in like the fog that crept out of the hollows. Fall is a time of endings, as nature wraps up the summer and battens down the hatches for the winter storms to come. On such days, it can be hard to stay cheerful. I am not naturally blessed with a sunny nature. I have to work at it. Sometimes, the cheer floods out of me as though someone stuck a nail in a water balloon. There's a whooshing noise, and then the bag deflates until nothing is left but a wrinkled old piece of pink elastic, good for nothing, useful to no one. In fact, worse than useless. You can't just leave that punctured balloon lying there shriveled up on the ground; you would be littering. You've got to pick it up and dispose of it somewhere.

A Green Heron came flying in, spread its wings, raised up its head feathers, and landed on the dead willow snag at the north end of the pond. For a moment it stood there, gloriously stretched out, tall and imposing. Then the bird shrank down its neck and slumped into the more familiar shape of hunched-up heron.

Its slump was not mine, however. Not for it the fruitless contemplation of the pointlessness of life. Nihilism? Existential angst? Metaphysical mysteries? Pah! That heron was there to fish.

Slowly the realization dawned on me that to truly understand nature and our place in it, we shouldn't ask, "What is the point?" That is the wrong question. For us, a better question would be, "What is the meaning?"

Meaning is something we create ourselves. It's original in each of us, and under our control. We can tell ourselves our own happy little story, or a sad one, for that matter. We can change the story as we ourselves change, or as we wish to change. Because we supply all the meaning to the events in our lives, we can actually change the past—not the events, but the interpretation, the lessons; in other words, the important stuff. We don't have to stay stuck in the same place, ever. Attitude is everything.

I remember listening to a Salish tribal elder give a talk to a group of seventh-graders. He began by telling the kids a fable about how the People lost the sun. "They decided to send a bird up into the sky to bring it back. Of course, the big birds bragged about how they were the only ones who could fly that far. So first, Great Blue Heron tried, but he got tired on the way up and had to return. Then Red-tailed Hawk tried, but he couldn't do it either. One by one, all the big birds failed. Finally, Robin said he would do it. All the People laughed at him. 'You're so small,' they said. 'Why do you think you can do something that the big birds can't do?'

"But Robin asked Eagle if he could ride on his back as far as Eagle could go. When Eagle flew as high as he could and started to sink back to Earth, Robin launched himself from Eagle's back and..." The storyteller stopped. He had noticed that the kids were restless and upset. "What's wrong?" he asked them.

The kids didn't want to answer at first. They squirmed in their chairs. Finally one boy said, "You're telling us a children's story, but we're not little children anymore." He sounded aggrieved that the storyteller would treat such mature adults as he and his colleagues with so much disrespect. The other kids nodded.

"Ah," said the storyteller. He thought for a while. Then he said, "When I was a child, I heard this story over and over again. In my lifetime, I've probably heard it a hundred times or more, but I never interrupted the storyteller as you have done. Do you know why?"

The seventh-graders were too embarrassed to answer, but one girl eventually guessed, "Because in your culture, kids are more polite to their elders?"

The storyteller laughed. "Perhaps. But that is not the reason. The reason I never interrupted a storyteller is that every time I heard the same story, it was never truly the same. It was a different story because I was a different person. When I heard about Robin as a child, to me it was a funny story about animals. When I was a teenager, I heard the story about how you can be a hero even if you're not the strongest or most powerful one. When I grew up, I heard the story about how you can't necessarily accomplish very much by yourself. You can do a lot more if you cooperate with others. Now that I'm an elder, I hear the story about how our accomplishments are built on the efforts of others."

The same is true for me every time I go to the Fill. When I watch the Green Heron on the ugly pond, I can tell many stories about it, each one with a different meaning. One of my favorites is, "This is the story about how the Fill is a symbol of great hope." The Fill was a dump once, but now it is the home of this most fabulous creature, the Green Heron. It means that humans can mess up the world, but humans can also fix up the world. It means that I can make a difference—I can choose to help fix things, as I did when I pulled Purple Loosestrife from the base of the very tree that the heron was perched on.

It means that people, no matter how chimpian we are in our desire for stuff, or how reptilian we are in our bloodlust to hurt each other, can be divine and noble, too. We can be better if we will ourselves to be so.

Scientists tell us that our brains are governed by an assortment of electrochemicals that act from time to time to produce a thought. I suppose, according to this theory, some thoughts are higher up on the atomic chart and others lower down. How else to explain the appeal of beer commercials? No matter. The scientists may be correct about their chemistry, but I don't believe their findings give us the excuse to cave in to base impulses. We don't have to allow our limbicly challenged brain to control our actions just because we're a collection of chemicals. I'd rather follow Katharine Hepburn's advice. As she told Humphrey Bogart in a scene from *The African Queen*, "Human nature, Mr. Allnut, is what we were put in this world to rise above."

She meant that life is good, if we choose to make it so. Life is beautiful, if we decide to see it as so. That is the real meaning of life. And the meaning that we give to our lives is the whole point.

27. What Kind of a Birder Are You?

Recent DNA studies have caused a big shakeup in the classification of birders. All appearances to the contrary, we now know that there are only two clades, and they probably split off very recently. Some scientists believe the common ancestor to have been the last-century birder Roger Tory, of the family Peterson, the first birder to invent a system of identifying birds in the field by eye, without the necessity of shooting them in order to get a closer look.

Although the two clades of birders are superficially alike in appearance—dull plumage designed to blend into the environment, acute optics, goofy headgear, good shoes—you can always tell them apart by their behavioral differences. One clade of birders prefers to rush swiftly through the ecosystem, spotting birds left and right, moving so fast that the birds don't have time to hide from view. The other clade more often chooses to amble, racing snails to a tie on a good day. The common names for these two types of birders are "flitters" and "sitters."

Flitters are the kind of birder you want on your team when your local Audubon society holds a birdathon fundraiser. The whole point of a birdathon is to find as many birds as you can in one 24-hour period. For every bird that's spotted, sponsors give a little money to Audubon. Flitters are never so happy as when they skid to a halt in the parking lot at a birding site, burst out of the car, fan out to spot every avis in sight, be it rara or otherwise, pile back into the car like college kids trying to set a telephone booth record, and burn rubber on their way to the next site.

In my experience, flitters often volunteer to be leaders of birding trips. I was with such a group on a bus trip to Falcon Dam during the Harlingen Birding Festival in Texas one year. The bus left town in the predawn and drove 70 miles to the dam. Most of us slept on the way. When the bus pulled into the first stop on the banks of the Rio Grande, the leaders crowded around the door. If you've ever seen video showing how competitive skydivers leave an airplane, you'll be able to imagine how those guides exited the bus. While the rest of us were rubbing the sleep out of our eyes and asking, "Are we there yet?" the leaders were calling out birds. "There's an Altamira Oriole," cried one. "Got a Green Jay," trilled another. "Black Vulture," warbled a third. "Muscovy Duck," sang the first.

There was a silence. Muscovy Duck was a good bird. Unfortunately, it was flying along the riverbank just across the river, on the Mexican side of the border. The leaders started muttering like bowlers trying to steer their ball to the sweet spot on the bowling pins. "Come on, come on, fly over here a little more." Flitters, it turns out, are almost always listers, and you can't count a bird on your North American list unless it's on the U.S. side, which means it's got to be closer than halfway across the Rio Grande.

I have mixed feelings about that trip. On the one hand, I do keep a life list of all the bird species I have seen, and it was great to add so many new birds to it. But as a birder, I am definitely a sitter. I do not rush my birding, and I do not race to identify whatever I see. I once took three days to drive from Illinois to my husband's folks' house in Iowa, a distance of 70 miles. The folks got so worried about my absence that they almost called the state patrol. When I finally arrived and told them I had been birding my way to their place, they simply could not believe their ears. How could anyone take three days to drive 70 miles? Why, a person could walk faster than that. I tried to explain that in new habitat filled with strange new birds, a birder cannot be expected to drive more than a hundred yards before stopping to try to ID something. It did not register.

One reason it takes me so long to bird anywhere is that I like to identify the birds myself, without anyone helping. If this means that I must stare through my scope at a plover on the beach for an hour, as I try to decide whether it is an American or a Pacific Golden-plover, so be it.* Another reason I am slow is that I get inordinate pleasure out of the thought that I am existing in the birds' habitat, not the reverse. I love the feeling that I am a part of the ecosystem, just one more piece of the foliage, and that the birds take me as such if I am patient enough.

I was patient enough at the Fill yesterday. At first sight, the Fill has become a quiet place. In the early fall, with the blackbirds gone and few swallows left, the Fill can appear to be almost bird-less. This is especially true now because the prairie-style fields are so overgrown with plants that you cannot see the ground. If you listen, however, you can hear birds in the fields, although it's almost impossible to see any.

This is just as true at the ponds, where the plants grow too thickly to see migrating shorebirds very easily. They are there, however. I found them while sitting on my camp stool at the north end of the Main Pond. Least Sandpipers were foraging busily, along with two Long-billed Dowitchers. The birds had all come down from the tundra, migrating in the night and finding at the Fill a place to

---

*Our two species of golden-plovers look remarkably alike in winter plumage. They both are a nondescript beige/brown/white. The diagnostic field mark that distinguishes an American Golden-plover in winter plumage from a Pacific Golden-plover is that the primary projection of the wings is noticeably longer in Americans than in Pacifics. The primary projection, by the way, is measured when a bird's wings are folded. It is the amount of distance that the tip of the primary feathers— the outermost flight feathers of a bird's wing—stick out past the tertial feathers, the wing feathers closest to the bird's body. When a bird folds its wings, the feathers fold up like a fan. Some feathers fold under, and others fold over in layers. The folded layer closest to the tail tip is the primary feathers. The next layer, lying over the primaries and partially covering them, is the tertials. You've got to stare for a long time through a spotting scope at the back ends of golden-plovers to figure out whether the primaries are sticking out a long way or a short way from under the tertials of a given bird. Hence my slowness while birding.

catch their breath and fuel up for the next leg of their journey. I try never to bother these birds because I figure they don't need me to make them fly any more than they already have to. Unfortunately, a Cooper's Hawk who did not share my philosophy swooped in and spooked the birds. They all flew up in a ball and went keening off into the distance. The Cooper's did not give chase. She would no doubt have loved a little bite of dowitcher, but only if one showed that it was too weak or sick to escape. Seeing that all the birds were healthy, the Cooper's perched on the dead willow tree at the pond's edge and fluffed up her feathers.

A Green Heron, unflapped by the hawk, glided leisurely over the water's smooth surface, which was creased only a little by a passing breeze. The heron landed on a woody branch that stuck out over the water and immediately did its famous disappearing act. I knew it was there. I was, in fact, looking right at it. But its deep green, mahogany, brown, and beige feathers blended in so perfectly with the shadowy leaves that the bird was almost impossible to see.

While my eyes strained to make the heron reappear, my ears were busy, too. I heard the rough-voiced chips of numerous Common Yellowthroats in the irises. The yellowthroats are songbirds that have bred here at the Fill over the summer. They were far too cautious to come out when a bird-eating hawk was near, but eventually the Cooper's flew off and all the warblers popped out to forage near me. Two Bewick's Wrens in the young willow wands behind my head were more discreet, but after checking me out for fifteen minutes, they too came into the open. Meanwhile, seven Wood Ducks paddled by, not even looking up when little flocks of shorebirds flew in formation over their heads.

Two of the shorebirds came in for a landing and turned out to be a Lesser Yellowlegs and a Long-billed Dowitcher. The Lesser Yellowlegs is a very good bird for the Fill. It's a long-legged harlequin decked out in polka dots and ready to leap into the sky at the least sign of trouble. This particular bird seemed to feel comforted by the presence of the dowitcher. It also seemed to like a flotilla of Mallards that had docked near my stool. As both shorebirds began to feed, a Ruddy Duck drifted in to join the crew. They were all so close I could hear them snuffling in the water as they searched for food.

Then I noticed that the Ruddy Duck was no longer snuffling. It was sneaking. Apparently, it had decided that the Long-billed Dowitcher was offensive in some way. When the dowitcher's back was turned, the duck moved in close and gave it a chomp. The dowitcher leaped out of the way, but not far enough. Again, the Ruddy Duck waited until the dowitcher's back was turned, and then snap! another bite. The duck didn't harass the yellowlegs, only the dowitcher. Evidently a personal feud.

As for the poor dowitcher, it must have been wearing the avian version of a "Kick Me" sign, because when it flew into the brush on the east shore to escape the duck, a Virginia Rail crept out and gave it a bite, too. The dowticher gave a startled "Kek!" and then looked around to see who else might want to pick on it. I shook my head. "Not me," I hastened to say. The bird eyed me suspiciously for a moment, then bent its head to feed. Peace descended once again.

Off in the distance where some conifers grow across the street from the Fill, I could hear a pair of Steller's Jays just coming out from their breeding purdah. They were ready to be raucous again. Jays get very quiet at the Fill when they're on the nest, and I had missed hearing their rough voices. It was good to hear them scolding as I sat there on the shore and felt the pulse of life beat all around me.

I wish I could have sat there forever.

28. Ignorance Is Bliss

Brown-headed Cowbirds are the Blanche Duboises of the bird world—they depend on the kindness of strangers. Female cowbirds never build their own nests. Instead, they watch while other birds build theirs. When the female of another species lays an egg, the female cowbird sneaks in, gets rid of the egg, and lays her own in its place. The soon-to-be foster parents usually don't recognize the substitution, so they brood the cowbird's egg along with theirs. Unhappily, the baby cowbird hatches before the other nestlings do. It is bigger and more demanding, so the clueless foster parents give it more food. Often, the other nestlings starve to death, and the foster parents end up with only the cowbird baby.

Each female cowbird can lay some 40 eggs per spring, so she hasn't got the time to be picky about choosing victims. Almost anyone will do. In Washington State, Brown-headed Cowbirds have parasitized dozens of species of songbirds.

Late summer or early fall at the Fill is when you see how successful the cowbirds have been each year. This September near the Wedding Rock, I saw a White-crowned Sparrow hopping along in the grass with a baby cowbird in tow. The cowbird was enormous compared to the sparrow, but that didn't deter the baby from following the sparrow all over the glade, begging for food. The frazzled parent would gather a beakful of food, stuff it into the cowbird, and then fly away. No sooner did the cowbird gulp down the food than it was off after the sparrow again, begging, begging, begging.

I don't know how the sparrow stood it. I've been fated occasionally to book a flight on a crying-baby airplane, on which every other row seems to harbor a parent traveling with a screamer. The constant grizzling of the babies begins to wear away your brain until you find yourself wondering what it would be like to blow the emergency hatch and float away. Your landing would undoubtedly be rough, but it might be worth it. I suspect the White-crowned Sparrow working so hard at the Wedding Rock would agree.

It isn't really kindness that causes the victims to care for the cowbirds' babies. It's agnotology. Agnotology is a concept invented by Robert Proctor, a Stanford history of science professor, who coined the word from the Greek *agnosis,* meaning lack of knowledge. Agnotology is the science of ignorance. Proctor realized that ignorance can be culturally produced and controlled. It can be created *on purpose.*

White-crowned Sparrows parasitized by female cowbirds have no culture, of course, and no control over their own ignorance. They aren't programmed to recognize that a baby cowbird is not their offspring. Their instinct tells them that any bird hatched in the nest is theirs and needs to be cared for. Sparrows can't help themselves. People, on the other hand, can but often don't.

You can see this everywhere, both in people's personal lives and in the wider culture. For example, I practice an extreme version of agnotology when it comes to car maintenance. I don't want to know anything about it and never did. Early in our marriage, I took my husband driving in my old Pontiac. It was an eight-cylinder behemoth bequeathed to me by my parents. As we drove around, my husband cocked his head and said, "It sounds to me like the engine is missing on two cylinders."

"I wouldn't be surprised," I responded. "It's been sounding like that for months."

My husband's eyes bugged out on stalks. "You mean you've been driving around on six cylinders and haven't done anything about it?!?"

"Lots of people drive six-cylinder cars," I replied defensively. "What's the big deal? Hey, I figure I could get down to four cylinders and still drive to work. As far as I'm concerned, with six cylinders going all at once, I'm still two cylinders ahead of the game." I neither knew nor ever wanted to know that car cylinders were not designed to operate as a multiple-redundancy system.

My husband was amazed by that level of ignorance. He couldn't understand how so much obliviousness could exist in the world. How can a person drive a car every day and not know a thing about how it works? Yet my own agnotology extends even further—to cell phones, computers, my oven, the new radio-clock on my dresser. It's a long list, all tools of daily life with numerous buttons I have never pushed and hope I never will.

We all have similar black holes in the universe of our brains, but few of us want to confront them. Confronting them means we would have to educate ourselves, and most of us have better ways to spend our time. We're happier as agnotologists.

This is very puzzling. You would think that embracing such a high degree of ignorance would long ago have taken us down a one-way street to an evolutionary dead end. I mean, if you had refused to know everything you possibly could about leopards, lions, venomous snakes, and rhinos out on the savannah back in the day, your genes would have exited the pool long ago. You gotta know about that stuff to survive, right? The constant push for more knowledge seems *inherently* good.

Agnotology can be highly functional, however. Take cell research, for example. If you are a cell researcher, there are fifteen scientific journals that are important sources of the newest research findings. To keep up with your field, you should read all of them. These journals published 3,456 articles in 2003. If you had spent half an hour reading each article, it would have taken you 1,728 hours to read them all. If you read for 40 hours a week, you would have spent more than 43 weeks doing nothing else. That would have left only nine weeks in the year for you to do any other work, and that's without taking a vacation.

This pace of publication has continued since 2003. So many articles are being written by so many people worldwide that a biologist couldn't get through them if she did nothing but read them 24/7. Scientific articles are being disgorged by the millions every year. What's a poor scientist to do? Luckily, agnotology comes to the rescue—you can choose to be ignorant of all but a few articles in your field and thus save yourself from both eyestrain and brain fatigue.

Agnotology is a blessing in other situations as well—just ask the bureaucrats who hug ignorance to their bosoms when called to testify during congressional investigations. The fact is, modern civilization is complex and multifaceted, so much so that no one person can be an expert in all of it. That's why we have specialists. I don't have to know when or how to repair my car, for example. I simply have to know that I should take my husband driving now and then. He will diagnose mechanical problems and either fix them himself or take the car to a mechanic. Yes, I will have to endure extreme eye-rolling, but I will also end up with a perfectly running car. Ah, ignorance.

Agnotology may be functional for another reason. Being a master of facts does not necessarily mean you are a possessor of wisdom. Knowing is *not* the same as understanding. On the contrary, knowing a lot can mislead you into believing you comprehend it all, and when you think you comprehend everything, you don't have to pay attention to people who disagree with you. The fact that they do disagree only goes to show that they are lesser mortals, mere quibblers and ankle-biters, who bite and quibble precisely because they cannot grasp the width and breadth of your own vast knowledge.

Now you've become an ideologue, and everything must bow before your ideology, including any ethical standards society may try to impose.

What is the result? "The foundation of any long-term, functioning ethical system," answers Seattle attorney and author David Balint, "is based on *external* standards. If the standards aren't external, then ethics is simply a matter of our own taste. Unfortunately, if you make up your own standards, they are going to be self-serving."

Balint goes on to describe how he uses external standards to check his own actions. "I always try to act ethically in my profession. If you're going to practice law ethically, in regard to other lawyers, to the system, to your clients, and to your partners, you have to constantly examine your own actions and ferret out the self-serving positions. It's difficult to do, but you have to try."

Why do I bring this up in the context of birding at the Montlake Fill? Because of the fragile relationship between the birds and their tiny island of habitat in a sea of human development. The Fill is not a large place, but it hosts a large number of people who want to enjoy its beauty. The Fill—and any other wild habitat, for that matter—succeeds as a natural area only so long as people respect the needs of the wildlife.

This does not always happen. For years, people have been sticking their fingers in their ears and chanting, "Loo, loo, loo, loo, I can't hear you," whenever environmentalists pointed out that unrestricted growth was destroying habitat and would have grave consequences some day. That day may have arrived at the Fill. This September has been the worst year for fall shorebird migration I have seen in more than 20 years of birding. In sixteen visits to the Fill this month, I have seen one Spotted Sandpiper, three Greater Yellowlegs, and four Western Sandpipers. In other years, that kind of total would be bad for a single morning, let alone an entire season. Songbird migration has been low as well.

Has the avian apocalypse arrived? I don't know. I think not yet. Shorebirds have been reported migrating along the outer coast and through the Kent Valley this fall, but numbers there are much reduced, too. It's clear that shorebirds are headed for trouble, along with many other migratory birds.

The precipitous drop in worldwide bird populations makes each individual bird all the more precious. All the more rare, too. The rarity attracts birders, who want to see these beautiful creatures. Sometimes, the birders in their enthusiasm harass the very birds they love so much, putting them under even more pressure. I've seen bird photographers at the Fill trample Savannah Sparrow nesting areas to get close enough to take a picture of a rare Lazuli Bunting. I've seen a group of birders chase an American Bittern from pond to pond to pond, trying to get a look at the poor creature, who became so harassed that it flew away south, never to be seen again. I myself went off-trail last April to see a Swamp Sparrow, even though signs are posted asking everyone to stay on designated paths. The field I trampled didn't seem very important; the bird I wanted to watch was. To my shame, I put my desires first.

How often does this happen? I'm not sure I want to know!

I do notice that when I am out looking at birds, the birds almost always know they are being watched. Some flee from observation, wasting precious time and energy that should be spent purely on migration. Even the birds that tolerate my presence react to the fact that I am there. I am often eyed with wariness as I sit on my camp stool trying to blend in with the background. And yet there I sit.

I tell myself I am not really hurting the birds. Yes, they avoid me. Yes, they change their behavior when I am there. But if I think I am having too deleterious an effect on a bird, I leave, even if I really, really want to see the bird.

I respect the wildlife in other ways, too. Many, many times I have waited on the path while a bird forages in my way or takes a dust bath. I wait until the bird has finished its business and clears the path before I walk down it.

But no matter how respectful or careful I am, I do disturb the birds. I hope not very much, but it is a slippery slope, especially when my brain is so adept at ignoring morality and rationalizing my own desires. I do so want to see birds, it's almost obsessive.

That's why I like to keep agnotology in mind. If I know that, like all human beings, I am capable of choosing ignorance over knowledge when it serves my purpose, then that insight into myself might help keep me honest. It might be just the off-switch I need, especially when I think about how often my brain tells me that what seems like fun also seems like the right and moral thing to do.

Stupid brain.

29. The Perfect Planet

Autumn at the Fill is a Renaissance painting come to life. Abundance is everywhere, as nature provides a cornucopia of bugs and seeds for the birds. The golden stems of grass bend in graceful arcs, heavy with grain. The crab apple trees are loaded with plump apples, each fruit a pale green with just a blush of red. Serviceberry trees offer up their clusters of deep-purple berries for any bird who cares to visit.

As in every such painting, the colors nearby are bright. The details stand out clearly, etched by the interplay of light and shadow. But in the distance, a haze turns the hills blue and blurry. It is all unspeakably lovely. I try to bird the Fill every day of this season, so as not to miss a single stroke of nature's paintbrush.

Yesterday was typical. The early morning sun filtered through the alder grove, gilding the leaves that were just beginning to feel the touch of fall. Little pockets of cold air clung to the dales, chilling my legs as I walked the Loop Trail. In the distance, Mount Rainier gleamed pink and gold in the predawn light, crowned with a lenticular cloud that beatified the summit like a halo. The air was too still and too cold to shimmer, but the cloudless sky promised plenty of heat by midday.

On the Main Pond, mist rose in a smoke-thin veil. I peered through its gently drifting lappets to see if anyone was home. I was hoping to see the juvenile Green Heron who took up residence on the Main Pond in August and who can often be found imitating a statue under the willow wands. With its green/brown/beige camouflage, the Green Heron can be very hard to see even in the best light; it was impossible to find in this day's halftone world of mist. Everything on the pond was smudged into a silvery gray.

My eye was drawn to the only movement on this canvas: a tiny ripple of perfect circles in the middle of the pond. Something had just dived beneath the mirror waters. I waited. In a few seconds, up popped the little diver, a Horned Grebe.

Horned Grebes don't really have horns, of course. In their breeding plumage, they have outrageous gold feathers that sweep upwards like the twisty horns of some exotic African antelope. This contraption sits atop a red neck and cheeks as black as pitch. The whole array is eye-catching, precisely to catch the eyes of potential mates. However, once breeding has occurred, the grebes begin to molt into a more conservative suit of plain black and white.

This particular grebe was in the middle of its molt. The soon-to-be definition of black on top, white on the bottom was in transition. What was going to be dark was still light; what would soon be light was still dark. The result was a vaporous swirl of grays, turning the bird into a living puff of smoke floating on diaphanous mist. Not a Renaissance oil painting, but a study in charcoal, as stunning in its monochrome as anything ever sketched by Leonardo.

From my perspective at the north end of the pond, the grebe was paddling squarely between two protrusions sticking up from the water. On my right was a tiny island of wooden snags and plants. On the left were four twisted pieces of rusted rebar, signs of the garbage dump that lies beneath the Fill.

The contrast between the ugliness of the rebar and the beauty of the islet was stark. It is a contrast I often find here at the Fill. Not just the rebar in the Main Pond, but rotting tires, rusting methane burners, large pieces of broken concrete, old beer bottles, and indestructible plastic can be found everywhere at this site.

It would be easy to draw a simple lesson from these scenes: Nature is beautiful; man-made things are ugly. Nature is good; man's works are bad.

No artist would draw that lesson, however. Artists have a more expanded view. When asked to define art, for example, Seattle artist

and teacher April Ferry says, "Art is not about pretty pictures. Ugly art is art, too—or what you or I might consider ugly. Do I think that Rauschenberg's toilet really is art? It's not my kind of art, but I know that it is art. Anything that evokes an emotional response is art."

I thought about that as my eyes drifted upward from the Main Pond to view more works of man: the new indoor gym at the southwest end of the Fill that displaced the nest burrows of Belted Kingfishers when it was built; the two giant cantilevers of Husky Stadium that bracket the football field where 70,000 fans gather on Saturdays in the fall to watch other people play games; the smokestack of the campus's heat plant rising like the middle finger of a giant hand. In the winter, the smokestack pumps steam and greenhouse gases into the atmosphere.

All these works certainly evoked an emotion in me, but not, I admit, anything happy. Art it may be, but not the kind of art I like to look at. Still, April Ferry is right. Art evokes emotion, and it also provokes thought. What better place than the Fill to think about human nature and our relationship to wild nature?

Philosophers, scientists, poets, and preachers have struggled for centuries to explain us to ourselves. What makes us human, versus animal, versus divine? The more that scientists understand the underlying chemistry, biology, and behavior of life on Earth, the less we humans can claim to be unique. And yet, there is that little voice inside us—our moms? our third-grade teachers? our own egos?—that keeps telling us we are special.

Without getting into an argument about the origin of our opposable thumbs and/or the nature of our immortal souls, it's useful to think about the fact that one of the major characteristics that defines us as human is our duality. We are individuals, yet we cannot survive alone—we need community. We build our own environments by creating cultural buffers between us and the natural environment, yet we are firmly embedded in nature, too. We are rational and can reason, using our highly developed cortexes, but our reptilian hind-brains exert enormous control over us as well. We exist in a constant push-pull on many levels.

The ancient Greeks likened our souls to two horses, one wild and one tame. Both were harnessed to one chariot. Greek philosophers said that if the chariot is to move forward, the charioteer must control our inner horses and get them to work together. In other words, as individuals and as a species, we do best when we keep all our contradictions in balance. Then our duality becomes our greatest strength, for then we have access to both sides of our nature and can use each side to its greatest, most productive extent. We do worst when we go to extremes, no matter what those extremes may be.

For example, the garbage that pops up from time to time at the Fill reminds us of the waste we generate as we go about our daily business. It tells us that we humans are perfectly capable of gobbling up more than our share of the world's resources, stuffing ourselves to gluttony and poor health, poisoning our atmosphere, exterminating other species. We make ugliness in the world. But we also make beauty. The Fill was created by us. We made the land come forth from the waters of the lake. We built up the rolling hills on mounds of garbage and landfill dirt. We set aside 75 acres to be used primarily for nature and only secondarily by us. The Fill is both ugly and beautiful, a dump and an Eden, a wild haven in the heart of a city, a contradiction that mirrors the push-pull within us.

Someone once said that our planet was perfectly designed for us. The temperatures are not too hot or too cold. The drinking water is fresh. The plants are edible. They provide all the nutrients we need to grow and stay healthy. Earth's flora, fauna, and even minerals can be made into shelter for us. The sun gives us just the right amount of energy, and at dawn and dusk, the full measure of beauty to feed our souls. It's all perfect.

The question is, are we perfectly designed for the planet?

With respect to nature, the immediate answer has got to be no. We are out of balance. You can see this everywhere—in global warming, species extinctions, the food crisis, the energy crisis, the water crisis, the loss of habitat, the spread of invasive species that we ourselves introduce. The dark forces of greed and overpopulation threaten to run away with us. But we are the charioteer, and we have the power to decide how to control our wild horses, or even if we will. We can bring us back into balance with the planet, if we choose. It is an empowering thought.

In his book *A Devil's Chaplain*, Richard Dawkins asked himself this question: What is a lion's natural habitat? It is the savannah, he said. Lions do best when they live in the savannah. Then what is our natural environment? he asked himself. To a very large extent, he said, it is ourselves—our relationships and our culture. Lions can do very little to change their environment. Certainly if something goes awry with it, lions are incapable of correcting what's wrong. But because we ourselves create so much of our environment, we do have the capability to alter it, either positively or negatively.

At the moment, we make many decisions that harm our natural world. We know this, but we do little to change our ways. We tell ourselves that the problems are too big, that one person cannot change the behavior of billions. We are each one drop in a vast ocean, and how much can one drop do? But this is specious reasoning. Collectively, our decisions about transportation, food, shelter, clothing, fun, work, and everything else that fills our lives are altering our planet for the worst. Why can't our collective decisions alter our planet for the best? Our rush to the edge of the cliff does not seem to me to be a given. We are humans, not lemmings. We have animal impulses, but we are not just animals. We are more. Abraham Lincoln called this added feature of humans "the better angels of our nature." On the eve of the Civil War, he called out to them. He knew they were in our hearts somewhere.

Pondering these issues as I sat at the Main Pond, I saw that the juvenile Green Heron had come out of hiding and was perched on the rebar. A short distance away, a Red-tailed Hawk had flown in and was perched on the wooden snag of the natural islet. Between them, the Horned Grebe dove again, stirring the veils of mist, smearing the outlines of the hawk and the heron.

The birds didn't care whether their environment was natural or man-made, ugly or beautiful. It was there, and it suited them. And we humans are responsible for it.

30. Fans

Science tells us that many species of migratory birds come to North America at the same time each year. San Juan Capistrano has its swallows *(Petrochelidon pyrrhonota)*, Othello in Eastern Washington has its Sandhill Cranes *(Grus canadensis)*, but nothing is more certain or more punctual than the fall appearance of large flocks of *Pedisballus fanus huskiensis* at the Montlake Fill.

Traditionally, the flock first appears on the first Saturday in September, decked out in its fall plumage of purple and white. Sometimes, the discerning birder can spot the occasional gold-crowned variant, but this is rare.

For some reason, when the flock arrives, it always arrives in huge numbers. By huge, I mean 70,000 individuals per flock, although of course it's hard to get an exact count. Suffice it to say that by noon, these birds literally cover the parking lot west of the Fill. All three subspecies are usually present: the large *P. fanus huskiensis winnebagus*, the smaller and more active *P. fanus huskiensis pickuptruckus*, and the slower-moving least, *P. fanus huskiensis hoofnfoot*.

I don't want to raise birders' hopes too much, but I'm pretty sure that this year, I saw an extreme rarity: a *P. fanus byusis*. This vagrant from Salt Lake City has blue and white plumage that can be very hard to distinguish from the more common purple and white of our local birds, but the light was excellent on this day, and I got a good look before the specimen flew off in the direction of the stadium.

Luckily, all three of our local subspecies tend to be more sedentary than their Utah cousins, so they're easy to observe. Typically, they

172

feed right out in plain view in the parking lot for several hours. I've noticed that they eat a similar diet as our crows: hot dogs, a little potato salad, chips, and fries. After they've picked their paper plates clean, they preen for a while. Then, at some mysterious signal that ornithologists have yet to determine, the whole flock rises as one and heads over to the stadium. There, they perch on the benches and call distinctively for a couple of hours, after which the flock disperses.

In short, this is football Saturday at the University of Washington, and fans are in full roar.

It always amazes me that 70,000 people are willing to sit on hard benches in all types of weather, watching 22 meaty guys bash into each other for a couple of hours. Meanwhile, there is one little ol' birder sitting on a camp stool out in the fields and marshes of the Fill, trying to identify some true wonders of nature.

I suppose I ought to feel grateful that our species does have diverse interests. As it is, the 70,000 walk quickly through the Fill, sticking to the gravel path and taking time for only a short glance or two at the nature that surrounds them. They are on a mission, and while they probably are glad enough of a chance to see an eagle or a wild duck in the middle of a city, their real purpose is to watch football. Thus, despite the fact that tens of thousands of football fans actually use the Fill, in the sense that they walk its paths, they leave behind a tiny ecological footprint.

The birds don't seem to mind the effects of a football Saturday, not the roar of the crowds nor even the martial music of the band, which you can hear clearly when the wind blows in the right direction. In fact, the birds get used to the presence of humans at this site. As long as people don't actively bother them, most of the birds go about their business unconcernedly. I think they do this because most of the people who use the Fill pay no attention to the birds, and those of us who do (i.e., the birders) don't hurt anyone. The birds get used to seeing us all pass by, and they forget that we are perfectly capable of eating them.

Newcomer birds aren't so sanguine, especially ducks. When ducks arrive from their breeding grounds in the north, they are highly skittish. They won't let you get within 50 yards of them before they flush and fly out of sight. Soon, however, they begin to notice that the resident ducks aren't flushing. Most of the old-timers don't even bother to lift their heads from under their tucked-up wings when I arrive at the Main Pond to gawk. The newcomer ducks begin to question themselves: "Am I being too cautious, too conservative, paranoid even? Maybe I ought to re-examine my beliefs."

By the third day after they have arrived, the newcomers are willing to give me the benefit of the doubt. They eye me warily as I pass by, but they don't flush. A few days after that, they are as ho-hum about humans as the most mellow of our local Mallards.

This phenomenon is one of the reasons why the Fill is such a great birding spot. Birds here let you get closer to them than anywhere else I know. This is especially true if you are willing to sit quietly in one place for at least fifteen minutes. That's enough time for the residents to decide you're harmless, and for incoming flyers to think you're part of the landscape.

Yesterday was typical. I was sitting on my camp stool at the north end of the Main Pond, hoping to see migrating shorebirds and passerines. The shore was jumping with birds, but most were merely House Finches and American Goldfinches that had congregated to eat the thistle seeds and Queen Anne's Lace still standing after the CUH's mower had done its work the day before. These finches are so common at the Fill that they are almost a nuisance to the birder who is trying to spot new species. You see movement, you glass it, and then you find it's just number 382 of the previous 381 finches you've already glassed.

My arms were getting tired from lifting my binoculars to my eyes so often, only to find another finch. I began to consider the idea of running out into the field, waving my arms, and shouting to scare off the birds. I wouldn't be breaking new ground by doing this. As a matter of fact, the UW actually hires a model-rocket man to fire off loudly whistling rockets to shoo away the Canada Geese from the baseball diamond because the geese make it so hazardous—and messy—to slide into third. I would be doing the same thing to the finches, only I wouldn't charge the university a cent. Such a deal.

Then I looked around guiltily. What was I thinking? I'm a nature lover, not a bird bouncer. Fortunately, nobody can see your thoughts, can they? Technology hasn't reached that point yet, has it? I realize the CIA probably reads my emails; the Seattle Police have set up eyes in the sky at the nearest intersection to catch drivers running red lights; and yes, the Safeway checkout clerks seem to know my shopping habits well enough to offer me coupons on my next purchase of cereal. But thoughts are still private, aren't they?

As I was debating this point, I heard a little warble in the bush not six inches from my head. A House Finch began to serenade me, soon joined by the bush's resident Bewick's Wren. A few American Goldfinches landed in the willow snag nearby and began to chime in. I was encircled by song.

Three years ago, I took four of my sixth-grade writing students to interview Gerard Schwarz, maestro of the Seattle Symphony. After we were done taping the interview, the maestro asked us if we would like to listen to the symphony rehearse. His assistant quickly said that she had arranged for us to sit in the third row of Benaroya Hall, but Mr. Schwarz was so enchanted by my students that he insisted we be seated onstage with the musicians. We sat in the percussion section next to the timpani player. Every now and then, as rehearsal progressed, Mr. Schwarz pointed his baton directly at our section. Although we had no instruments to play, we felt a part of this vast and thrilling instrument, the Seattle Symphony. Just so did I feel that I had become a part of the birds' chorale, too. It was celestial.

We humans place a high value on uniqueness. A one-of-a-kind object is worth far more in our eyes than something that's mass produced in large quantities. This is true even when the object is a mistake. In 2005, for example, a four-stamp plate block of the inverted "Jenny" (a 1918 two-color airmail stamp in which the blue Curtiss JN-4 airplane in the center of the design was inadvertently printed upside down) sold for almost $3 million. The stamps themselves had a face value of 96 cents. There are many other examples of this bias: The ball that Mark McGwire hit for his 70th home run sold for $3 million. A Canada Goose decoy carved by master decoy-artist A. Elmer Crowell brought in $684,500. A Navajo blanket with woven stripes was appraised at $350,000 to $500,000.

Our bias toward uniqueness is evident in birding, too. Many of us chase rarities, and here in the Northwest, we post our unusual sightings on Tweeters, our Internet bulletin board. I'm among the guiltiest. My biggest chase was when I hopped on a plane and flew all the way across the country to Martha's Vineyard to see North America's first Red-footed Falcon. That was in August 2004. (As an aside, it was totally worth it, and if you ever, ever get a chance to see a bird that's a first North American record, mortgage your firstborn and go. You won't be sorry.)

Dennis Paulson, who has taught Seattle Audubon's master birder classes for years, is well aware of this bias. That's why he always tells his students, "Look at every bird." There's no telling when a bird we think is common turns out to be rare—and hence, more valuable.

I've often said that if we truly have descended from more primitive animals as the evolutionary biologists say, we would have been far better off if we had chosen cows rather than chimps to be our ancestors. Cows are so placid. They live in herds, and they all get along. They don't compare who has the biggest blade of grass to chew. They're content to chew whatever cud comes their way. Cows don't seek out fields that have one rare blade of grass. They prefer fields with abundant fodder. The more food, the better, is their view. Chimps, on the other hand, are always on the lookout for the one who has the last, biggest banana. The chimp who does possess this rarity is the Alpha, and all look up to him or her. They stand in line to groom the Alpha. Secretly, they all wish they were the Alpha, so they could have the last, biggest banana themselves.

It doesn't have to be this way. Maybe instead of valuing the rarest of items, we should value the ordinary, everyday stuff. It would certainly be better for the environment if we did. For example, if people back in the 1800s had valued the Passenger Pigeon, which once numbered as many as five billion birds, perhaps we would still see today their migratory flight, when a flock a mile wide took hours to pass overhead. If people had valued the Whooping Crane when it was more common, perhaps we wouldn't be expending extraordinary efforts to save the species today. Ditto for the California Condor, Kirtland's Warbler, and a host of native Hawaiian birds, including the Nene and the Alala.

Placing the highest value on the ordinary might be better for our work lives and our families, too. If we valued the ordinary, then we wouldn't invest so much hope in the perfect holiday, thus producing stress, which in turn produces unhappiness, which in turn ruins the perfection of the holiday. The perfect holiday would be every day. Similarly, the perfect love of our lives would be the man we married, thinking he was Sir Galahad but realizing after years of picking up his dirty socks that he is ordinary and needs some fixing up. But if we realized how valuable such an ordinary person is, then he would indeed be a superhero, and the very best kind: everyday.

I suspect all those Husky fans know this simple lesson about how to lead the good life. While it is true that the stadium erupts when a great and rare play is made, and we are all proud when our team goes to the Rose Bowl after a successful season, it is also true that if the team is in the tank, the fans still come to watch the games. They come to enjoy football and each other, no matter what.

I ran into a birder friend, Zsolt Farkas, yesterday as he was coming from the Fill. "Anything good here today?" I asked him.

"Oh, yes," he replied. "There is the most wonderful flock of American Goldfinches feeding on the thistles near Shoveler's Pond. There must be a hundred of them or more. They're fantastic."

Actually, the goldfinches were in their drab winter plumage, a kind of dull mustard and black. They were cheeping, not singing their beautiful songs, and they've been there for the past several weeks. All the birders visiting the Fill pass them by after scarcely a look. But Zsolt reminded me what the real secret of happy birding is: it's all good. For him, as for me, the ordinary is the extraordinary because nature is full of everyday wonder—including the wonder of a chorus of common House Finches on the Main Pond, quietly warbling just for me.

31. A Tale of Loss

Once upon a time, there was a beautiful, young Bald Eagle who found a good territory for himself on the shores of Lake Washington near the Montlake Fill. The eagle discovered that fish were plentiful in his new home, and the crows didn't pester him too much. If you're an eagle, you can't ask for better than that.

When the sun rose over the foothills of the Cascades in the east and turned the waters of the lake to molten gold, the eagle liked to perch on the dead snag at the point, where he could survey his territory and make sure that other eagles weren't horning in. Whenever he got hungry, he would spread his wings, catch a little thermal updraft, and soar over the lake, using his sharp eyes to detect fish near the surface. As soon as he spotted one, he would fold up his wings, plunge down like a missile, and grab the fish with his talons. Sometimes the fish was so big the eagle couldn't lift it. So he would flap his way over to a log in the bay, dragging his fish along underwater. He looked like a water-skier without a boat. At the log, he would haul his fish partway out of the water and eat it right there.

Life at the Fill was very good for the eagle, but after a while, he became lonely, if eagles can ever be said to feel loneliness. At the very least, he felt there was something missing in his life, but being an eagle and not a psychologist, he couldn't articulate what it was.

Then one day, a young female eagle appeared in the skies over the Fill. She soared high above the male's territory, her wings spread out straight and strong, her white head and tail gleaming in the sunlight. Although she was only a tiny speck in the distance, the male eagle saw her at once. Eagles don't need binoculars to see faraway things, and of course, the male was always on the lookout for intruders.

As soon as he saw her, he sprang into the sky to chase her off. But when he got close, he lost all desire to attack. Instead, he and she began the age-old dance of the eagles, a tango among the clouds— now near, now far, now circling, now straight. As the male eagle dove past her one last time, she taunted him with her strength, and dared him to court her, and so he turned upside down and locked talons with her. The joined eagles tumbled from the sky, rolling over and over as they fell, but neither would let go. They disappeared behind the hills and no one saw what happened next. The eagles were alone together.

A few days later, the male eagle flew over to Foster Island, where the winter winds had blown down many trees. He selected a big branch, longer than he was, and heavy, and he picked it up with his strong talons and flew over to a place called Talaris, where the tall cottonwood trees grow. There he dropped his branch, and it lodged in the crotch of one of the biggest trees. That was the eagle's first branch. Soon his mate arrived with another limb and dropped it near the first one. It, too, lodged in the tree, and so the two eagles gradually built their nest.

When it was ready, the female lined the nest with soft feathers and leaves, and she laid two eggs. She was tired after that, and glad when her mate brought her a fish to eat.

Throughout the early spring, the two eagles took turns sitting on the nest, keeping the precious eggs warm and protecting them from marauding crows. In time, the eggs hatched, and two ugly babies began keening for food. The eagles became very busy then, catching fish and stuffing the babies' mouths, which never seemed to be satisfied.

In a matter of a few weeks, the babies began to sprout real feathers instead of down. They grew so big that they could no longer fit in the nest together, so they climbed to the top of the nest and teetered on the edge while they flapped their wings to gain strength. The parents could often be seen perched nearby, standing watch. Occasionally, the adults would leave the babies alone while they went off to hunt. When the parents judged that the babies had become big and strong enough to leave the nest, they began to spend less time fetching food and more time out of the babies' view. Hunger, for eagles, is a great motivator, and gradually the babies began to get the idea that maybe they should find their own food.

One day, the biggest baby was performing his flapping exercise and, much to everyone's amazement, lifted off the nest and managed

to flop onto a nearby branch. Shortly after that, the babies were ready to fly away altogether and become eagles on their own.

The two parents left the nest as well and went their separate ways, but only for a short while. When the cool weather and clouds of late fall returned, the two eagles came back to the Montlake Fill and renewed their bond. As the days grew shorter and winter advanced, the eagles danced in the sky again and locked talons and started a new family.

And so the happy years passed. Every winter, the male eagle and his mate added a few new sticks to their nest, and every spring they raised a little brood.

But then one fall, the female did not return to her mate as she used to do. For weeks, the male eagle sat on his perch with his bill pointed up, using his powerful eyes to scan the empty sky. Sometimes he would spread his great wings, catch a rising thermal, and soar high above Lake Washington, looking for her. But she never returned. He was alone.

What thoughts did the eagle think? What grief did he feel? People say that animals have no deep emotions. They say that animals cannot love, or laugh, or mourn. So I do not say that the eagle grieved for his mate. I do not say that he missed her beautiful wings or remembered her taunting challenge to tango above the foothills. Eagles can't cry tears, but every now and then, he would cry a great cry, calling for his mate. The cry would rise up to the heavens and expand to reach the far clouds, but it could not reach the place where the female eagle had gone, for she was no more.

Instinct told the eagle to keep hunting for fish, to preen his feathers and clean his talons, to soar when the air grew warm, and to avoid the crows who sometimes pestered him. Life goes on, and so did the eagle. But it was not the same. Two had become one, and the eagle never again carried a branch back to his nest.

I sometimes think that the biggest curse of being human lies in our big brains that can store almost infinite amounts of memory. We remember those who have left us, and we carry the knowledge that they will be with us no more on this Earth. The loss weighs upon us, a burden so heavy that we can only bow our necks in grief. We cannot see the sunlight then or the birds or the other beauties all around us. And our tears rain down.

How can we go on in the face of such sorrow?

At the far end of the field that stretches south from the Center for Urban Horticulture lies fallen a great cottonwood tree, stretching out more than 40 feet on the ground. I remember the day it fell. Seattle tends to experience mild weather all year long, but every now and then, usually in the fall or winter, a storm blows in with hurricane-force winds. The power goes out in thousands of homes, the last leaves of autumn that had been clinging tenaciously to the maples fly off, and some of the great tree-giants that had withstood so many previous storms finally succumb.

So it was with the cottonwood tree that had stood so tall on the edge of the field. When the wind blew down that tree, the giant did not die right away. For some time, it continued to put out leaves and provide shelter for birds. But gradually, it lost its life force, until finally it passed away and was a tree no longer.

Few now remember that tree. Its trunk lies covered by blackberry bushes and ivy so thickly that no one can see that it was ever a tree. I know it's still there because I remember, but when I tell my birder friends that a great tree lies hidden under the brush, they look at me in disbelief.

I suppose you could say that the cottonwood was just a tree, and there are still many, many trees at the Fill. Some of them are even growing where the cottonwood once did. I suppose you could also say that the cottonwood had a good, long life before it fell, that it is nature's way for the old to die and make way for the young. All of this is true, though of small comfort. I miss my tree.

Then one day, as I sat on my camp stool near the fallen tree, an unusual sparrow popped up out of the thicket that covers my companion. I know the Song Sparrows who live here year-round, the occasional Lincoln's Sparrows who visit in winter, the Fox Sparrows who prefer the blackberries east of the greenhouses and turn up about twice a month at the cottonwood tree for a quick forage, but I did not know this stranger. It had rusty-colored wings, rich buff on its breast and flanks, a gray-striped face, and a white throat.

The sparrow turned one way and then another, giving me long, full views from all angles. Then it gave a little trill and disappeared back into the brush. I knew then that I had just seen a Swamp Sparrow, a very rare bird for the Fill. It was so beautiful that joy filled my soul, replacing my sense of loss for the tree that had been here so long but was now gone. I beamed.

Lately, I have been thinking about the story of Job in the Bible. Job, you may recall, was a righteous, God-fearing man, a pillar of his community, happily married, with ten children. Unfortunately, he became a pawn in a game played by God and Satan. Satan claimed that the only reason Job was pious was because God had given him wealth, prestige, and happiness. "Take those away," said Satan, "and Job will curse you."

So God told Satan to do his worst, and Satan destroyed all of Job's wealth, and all his children. Still Job was faithful, and God told Satan, "See, what did I tell you?"

But Satan thought for a second and answered, "Yeah, Job's still pious because we didn't attack him personally. But if something bad happened to his own body, then he'd curse you for sure."

So God gave Satan permission to harm Job himself, and Satan proceeded to afflict Job with boils and disease. Still Job remained faithful. He did question why these misfortunes were happening to him, going so far as to curse the day he was born, but he never succumbed to the temptation to curse God. In the end, God decided to reward Job by making him even wealthier than before. He also gave Job ten new children, including three daughters who were the most beautiful in the land. And Job lived happily ever after.

It has always bothered me that when God rewarded Job for his piety, He gave him ten new, even more beautiful children. Having lost loved ones myself, I know that no one can ever replace them, even if you get new ones who are a beauty-upgrade from the old ones. Who cares about what your loved ones look like? People aren't coins to be repaid or replenished. Each person is unique, and uniquely loved. In my opinion, since God did not give back to Job all that he had allowed Satan to take away, God did not restore Job to his former happiness.

But that's not the point of this story, I have come to realize. Life is not set up to be fair or just. It's not even set up to be understood in those terms. No matter how hard we try, or how good we try to be, we will lose people we love. We will suffer blows that we do not deserve. We will endure pain and trouble that we cannot avoid. When these things happen, nothing in life will replace what we have lost. Life without our beloved will never return to its same path. We can, however, love again. Just as the cottonwood tree sheds its leaves in the fall, it can grow new ones in the spring. And if the cottonwood tree itself falls, new life will spring up in its place. It won't be the same life, but we can find a new kind of joy in it.

As for the ones who have left us forever, our memories of them live on. Who they were, how they were, the things they did—these can never die as long as we hold them in our hearts. The ways they affected us continue to affect us. The gifts they gave to our spirit are not diminished but keep enriching us. "Death is but crossing the world, as friends do the seas," said William Penn. "They live in one another still... This is the comfort of friends, that though they may be said to die, yet their friendship and society are, in the best sense, ever present, because immortal."

The eagle was not gifted with a big brain to treasure the memories of his mate, but we are. We can remember the best and the worst that happens to us. If we let the memories of the worst flood our soul, then we suffer again and again the pain of loss. If we imagine the might-have-been, our memories will torture us with regret for lost opportunity. But if we bring back the memories of the best that was embodied in our love, then the goodness lives on in us. And in that sense—Penn's best sense—our loved ones are with us always.

32. A Winter Wren in Fall

Birding is as much a listening skill as it is a visual one. Really skilled birders can identify hundreds of species by song alone. The great birders can even identify the little chipping noises that birds often make when they're hopping around doing their birdly business but can't be bothered to break into song.

It is said that Roger Tory Peterson, the preeminent birder of the 20th century, was lying in bed one day near Cobb's Island, Virginia. His birder friends had left him alone while they went out at the crack of dawn to find as many birds as they could. When they got back, Peterson asked them which species they had found. It turned out they had found 42 species by tramping all over the place, while Peterson had "found" 40 just by lying still and listening.

Birding by ear is not a skill I have developed very far, I'm sorry to say. Part of the trouble is that many bird songs sound alike to me. This issue came up repeatedly when I took Seattle Audubon's master birder class. The lecturer would play a song sung by a Hammond's Flycatcher, for example, and one sung by a Dusky Flycatcher and say, "Can you hear how different they are?"

Hearing the difference in their songs is crucial because in the field, Hammond's and Dusky look almost identical. Only the song differentiates them diagnostically.

Everyone in the class would nod, except for me. I would scrunch up my face as I listened to the replay, hoping somehow that the added blood flow to my ears would increase their acuity, but all it ever seemed to do was turn them red.

Part of the trouble is that even when I can hear the differences in a given song, the song doesn't seem to stick in my brain. It gets in there amongst the brain cells, resonates around the synapses for a while, and then exits, stage right, leaving no trace. I can sometimes vaguely remember that I might have heard a song before, but I can't be sure. Maybe it's a brand-new song, and I'm just having a senior moment. As I get older, I find that manufactured memories are just as good as real ones, and since most of my friends can't remember anything either, it doesn't matter to any of us. We thus expand our experiences without bothering to have them first. Very convenient when trading stories at the coffee klatch, but not very effective when trying to identify birds in the field.

A lot of the birding books suggest mnemonics can help. The Yellow Warbler, for example, is supposed to sing, "Sweet, sweet, sweet, I'm so sweet," according to National Geographic's *Field Guide to the Birds of North America.* This book also quotes the Olive-sided Flycatcher as singing, "Quick-three-beers."

I suppose if I could hear these birds say those mnemonics, it might help, but when I listen to them sing, I don't hear them speaking English. I hear trills and whistles and buzzes that bear no resemblance to any human language. And realistically, even if I could discern the words, could I remember that it's the warbler that has an eating disorder and the flycatcher that's boozing it up? I have my doubts.

So I was quite proud of myself one day in fall when I heard a very loud chipping noise coming from the alder grove near the Center for Urban Horticulture, and I thought it sounded like a Winter Wren. Winter Wrens are little brown birds with ridiculously tiny tails and long, pointy bills that they use to probe through leaf litter to find insects and spiders. They also like to hop along branches and fallen logs, picking up bugs one by one. Contrary to their name, Winter Wrens do not confine themselves to winter in our state; they're here year-round, although they don't often stay for long at the Fill.

This wren seemed happy to be here, perhaps because there was plenty to eat. It busily hopped around in the bushes at the base of one tree, then flew over to another tree to forage, all the while making the kind of call note that caused Native Americans to name it "little bird with the big voice." Its chip sounded like it was speaking through a wren-megaphone. I quietly unfolded my camp stool and sat down to watch.

As so often happens, I was the only person around, and as also happens, I soon began to feel that I had left my own world behind and had entered the wren's world, a place where every plant presented a cafeteria of hors d'oeuvres. Here a grub, there a midge, over here a little worm. It was enough to make anyone chip for joy.

Entering the birds' world is a magical experience for me, and one of birding's greatest appeals. I can do it only if I let go of my worries, stop living in the past or the future, and just be still. It takes conscious effort to do this because it means that I have to give up one of my most human attributes: the ability to plan for the future.

Planning, I'm convinced, is one of the few things left on a list of "what makes humans unique." That list is an ever-diminishing one, thanks to Jane Goodall, Frans de Waal, and other modern zoologists, who have learned that other apes make war, have bad relatives, and play jokes on each other. It's not opposable thumbs, toolmaking, language, singing, building, cooperation, individuality, or even free will that set us apart from animals. Other creatures have these things, though usually not to the degree that we do. (My cat, on the other hand, has bunches more free will than I'll ever have.)

Long-term planning, though, is very human. Oh, I know that Frans de Waal has documented chimps carrying little twigs for a surprising distance in anticipation of fishing for termites. But this is mere preparation, not long-term, strategic thinking. The chimps know when the termites are ready to emerge from their rock-hard mounds because the termites make soft emergence tubes that the chimps can probe. The chimps arrive with their fishing-twigs, but they're on an *immediate* mission: must eat termites. This preparation, while impressive, is rudimentary. Real long-term planning takes worry, and our worry centers are the largest of any known creature. Mine are especially well developed.

When my worries begin to get the better of me, I go to the Fill to find peace of mind. I can't get to this state if I'm moving fast, so I amble. Some of my faster-paced birding friends say that watching me bird is like watching paint dry. They prefer to walk briskly along, catching sight of every bird in the land before the birds are even aware that someone is about to spy them out. Most of my friends thus see more birds than I do, but that's okay. I'm not out there just to bird. Or maybe it's more accurate to say that birding for me is not just about finding as many birds as I can. It's about finding something else.

To me, nature is a place where I go to renew my joy, regain my strength, and count my blessings. On especially good days, I feel a kind of oomph inside my heart as my spirit struggles to fly up on the wings of the beautiful birds. Something in me bursts forth into the sky, and I feel such joy that it is too big to contain. It speeds outwards like waves of solar plasma and bathes the Fill like the *schöner Götterfunken,"* in Friedrich Schiller's "Ode to Joy," a bright spark of the gods. Beethoven might as well be conducting his Ninth Symphony right there in the alder grove, along with that little tenor, the Winter Wren.

At such times, do I feel at one with nature? Gosh, no. How could I, sitting on my plastic and metal stool from REI, holding my plastic and glass binoculars from Nikon, and wearing my who-knows-made-from-what running shoes from some knockoff company in Southeast Asia? But I do feel at peace in nature. And that is quite enough.

Part V
Appendices

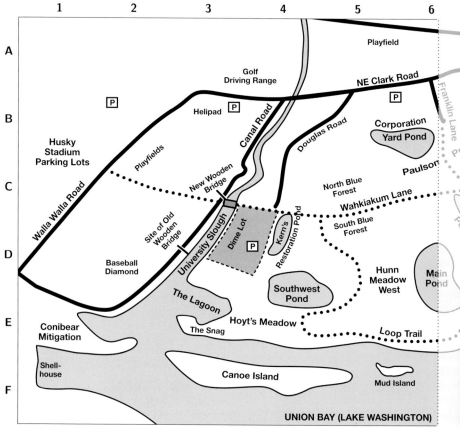

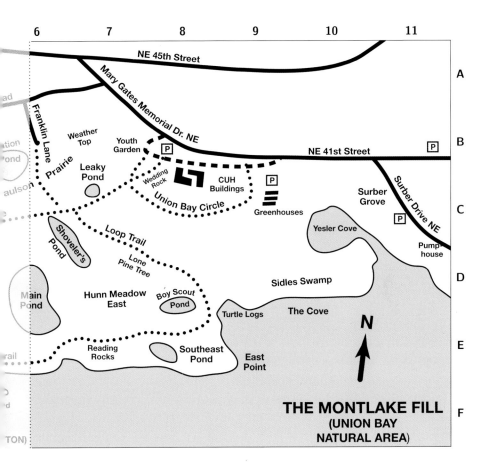

A. Montlake Fill History

Before the Montlake Fill became the Fill, it lay under the waters of Lake Washington. In 1916, the Ship Canal connecting Lake Washington to Puget Sound was opened, and the lake was lowered eight feet nine inches. When that happened, the Fill emerged from the lake bottom and became an extensive peat bog, marsh, swamp, and mudflat stretching from the Burke-Gilman Trail on the west and north to Mary Gates Memorial Drive NE on the east.

Most of the newly emerged land south of NE 45th Street was automatically held by the University of Washington. This was because when Washington became a state in 1889, the federal government granted a section of land—Section 16, specifically—to the state for charitable, educational, or penal purposes. In 1895, the city fathers of Seattle asked the state to allow the University of Washington to move to Section 16 because its site in downtown Seattle was getting too crowded. The legislature agreed. Part of Section 16 was underwater. When the lake was lowered, the added acreage increased the size of Section 16 and thus the university's holdings. However, the land was not usable for development because it was too marshy.

Back then, people had no use for such wasteland, beyond a little fishing. So when the City of Seattle approached the university and asked to lease part of the marsh to create a dump and a landfill, the university jumped at the chance. For the university, the deal was irresistible. The city would pay the school to fill up the area with garbage and construction dirt, and eventually, the university would own new-made land, prime real estate in the heart of Seattle.

In 1926, the first dump opened. Trucks began bringing in household garbage, as well as rubbish, ash, stumps, and construction rubble. The city allowed individuals to dump household waste as well. At the height of operations, as many as 110 truckloads of garbage were brought in daily. During one spring cleanup, 2,500 private vehicles brought their yard waste to the dump in a single day. In 1956, the garbage part of the operation began to function as a sanitary landfill, meaning that each night, a contractor covered the day's garbage with a layer of dirt.

In 1966, the active landfill began to close. The process was a gradual one, not completed until 1971. As different parts of the landfill closed, they were developed in various ways. A chunk of the northern part became playfields. A big portion of the western side became a giant parking lot for the university. Other portions were capped by a thin layer of clay and soil and seeded with grass.

When the site closed completely in 1971, there was great disagreement about how the remaining open spaces should be used. The College of Forestry wanted to plant study plots. The Urban Horticulture Center wanted a new building and demonstration gardens. The Athletic Department thought soccer fields would be ideal. One university official believed the land would make a great nine-hole golf course, with an adjacent faculty retirement center. (The golf driving range near the helipad is a remnant of this idea.) Meanwhile, the community wanted a park. The environmentalists thought a nature reserve would be best.

In 1976, the university created a committee led by Professor Richard Walker to figure out what to do. With financial support donated by the Northwest Ornamental Horticultural Society, the committee commissioned a study by the landscape architecture firm of Jones & Jones. The master plan they wrote recommended that the site be kept as an open natural area for the study of horticulture, landfill conversion, and nature. On May 13, 1977, the university's regents approved the Union Bay Arboretum Master Plan, setting aside a substantial portion of the landfill to be kept as a natural area.

Now known as the Union Bay Natural Area, the site is approximately 75 acres, administered by the College of Forest Resources and the UW's Botanic Gardens (which administers both the Washington Park Arboretum and the Center for Urban Horticulture). It is bordered by Lake Washington on the south, University Slough on the west, NE Clark Road on the north, and Surber Drive NE on the east.

A narrow portion of wetlands on the western side extends south as far as the Montlake Cut, skirting Husky Stadium. Another finger of wetlands extends north along University Slough to NE 45th Street.

The original master plan recommended that a big part of the landscape remain grassland and open ponds, favoring prairie birds and shorebirds, two of our most endangered avian groups. However, over the years, the site has become much more mixed. Today, it can best be characterized as a site of micro-habitats: some ponds, some prairie, a little marshland, a bit of swamp, a growing amount of riparian habitat, athletic fields of sod, and garden areas. Every little pocket of habitat is a bit different, and every one hosts its own collection of wildlife. More than 240 species of birds have been spotted at the Fill since recordkeeping began. Some birds are year-round residents, others are migrants, and a few are rarities that stay for a short time and then disappear.

The site experiences mixed use by humans as well as birds. Thousands of people come to the Fill each year to conduct nature studies, jog, fish, paint, ride bikes, stroll the baby, walk the dog, fly miniature airplanes, bird-watch, and get inspired. The art students who work at the ceramics building on the northeast side of the site use the Fill for artistic inspiration. Engineering students practice surveying. Athletes train. Restoration ecology students work on ridding the Fill of invasive plants and replacing them with native species.

For both humans and birds, the Fill is a dynamic place that changes every day, but one thing does not change: the Fill has the capability to open a door for us into nature, and thus it has the power to transform our everyday lives into wonder.

B. Inspiration

The other day, I was walking along Union Bay Circle when I heard a cyclist behind me. I turned to see a young boy barreling toward me as fast as he could pedal, his face filled with glee. I knew why. He had spotted the giant puddle that collects here in winter. Before I could get out of the way, boy and bike hit the puddle at full speed. Brown water spouted in every direction, drenching us both. Then the boy disappeared laughing down the road.

As I stood there dripping, I realized that he and I had both been inspired by the wonder that is the Fill. The boy was inspired to wreak havoc, not out of mean-spiritedness but just for the sheer fun of splashing. I was inspired to wish for those days of yesteryear when I would have been spry enough to catch that kid and give him a piece of my mind.

I laugh about that incident now, but there is a serious lesson to be learned, too. People come into nature for different reasons, and thus nature fulfills us in different ways. Such fulfillment can be conceived as a two-way exchange. We get something from the encounter, but we also give something back. This happens because we are changed by what we experience in nature.

For many of us, the gift we give back is a creative one. During the past year, I have asked many people at the Fill to contribute a work of art inspired by the nature they find here. The pages that follow contain their responses. I hope as you look through these pages that you, too, might be inspired to go out into nature and then create something from your encounter.

I also hope you will see, as I have, that a place like the Fill cannot exist unless a community of people commit themselves to create and maintain it. I believe if we each hold such a wild place in our hearts, then we will value it enough to keep it wild and free forever.

Who Eats?

a prose poem by Amy Davis

My list of chores to do grows longer, until most of my life is on it. Every morning, chased by guilt, I go to the lake, visit the birds, wait for hawks. On the trail to the marsh, the list drifts away. Wandering through the feathered world, the burdens of chronic illness fade.

Today, as I wait, a piping call fills the meadow. Two bald eagles hover above, knife-blade eyes fixed upon me. If I were smaller, I could have been breakfast.

The scent of wet hay covers the fields. Yesterday the grass was cut, the long golden tresses mowed down, yellow lotus and purple vetch clipped and gone for the season. Above the fields, the eagles prowl for lunch and dinner. They circle the sky in languid rings, swoop down on a terrible wind. I pray for the seven tiny ducklings I saw with their mother—so young and fluffy; believing in life, bathing in sun, pecking the mud for bugs all morning. But what do I know? What do I know of a life with wings—who eats, who doesn't?

All I know is when it's time to leave. Slowly, I walk away, cross the trails, wander in the cinnamon gardens. What do I know of a life with wings? All I know is when to be silent; when to sit still. When just one step will send them dashing away on toothpick legs, into the pond, away from the crunching steps of the brown-haired one. The brown-haired one who stands for hours, then turns without eating one worm, one bug, without drinking one flower. The one who could eat them but never does. The one who comes for only their presence. Why does she come? Why does she leave? What does she eat?

Each night at dusk, too late for guilt, I return, as mists spread across the fields and heron's wings close the horizon.

The Lone Pine Tree, by Doug Plummer

Green Heron, by R. L. Kothenbeutel

Strange Gardens, Companions

by Carlo Levy

Listening shadows,
our hidden worlds
inside each other,
words in our eyes
became old letters,
flowers gone to seed
in the garden
hospital, opened
memory schedules
for the bees
and trains to spring.

Pelicans flew over the sand,
roots and twisting stems
of the wild strawberries
holding down the sandclocks,
breathing the past,
the car far away
across the dunes, the men
and women of the ocean
muffled inside sunlight.

A hummingbird
in the damp, fall
camellia blossoms,
by a window,
located our rooms
in unknown places outside,
for the always changing
dreams missing, gaining
portions of the night.

I remember the curious
passages in summer
letters collecting
in a world
of endless dreaming
where no one reaches home
before waking in the morning.

We walked by the herons
of the lake standing
near old garbage mounds,
now a sanctuary of poplars,
eagles, wild carrot,
swallows, chicory, a car
waiting to be recognized
by our dog.

Marsh Wren, by Zsolt J. Farkas

Tree Swallows, by Gregg Thompson

Curious Cattle Egret, by Caren K. Park

A Place for Inspiration

by J. Lawrence Howard

When I first arrived in Seattle in 1961, the Montlake Fill was anything but a place for inspiration. My first and lasting impression was that it was a sea of mud and a cacophony of sounds, with rumbling heavy equipment and one million seagulls. In 1971 I found myself owning a home just up the hill. By then the landfill had been covered over, and staff were in the process of planting cover grasses. With decomposition, we had the ongoing show of methane flames shooting sky-high. As time passed the flames died out, and the land settled in some places and rose in others. Small depressions were places for methane to accumulate. In the evening we would toss a lighted match into one of them and be wonderfully startled by the whoosh of the gas burning in a flash.

Years passed and the area became something we just drove by. But then it came time for each of my sons to do their Eagle Scout projects. Who would have guessed that they would all want to do a project at the Center for Urban Horticulture (albeit with a bit of encouragement!)?

Because of the Scout projects, my relationship with the Fill grew. I now find it to be a place of relaxation, inspiration, and enjoyment. I walk the trails, count birds and turtles, take pictures of flowers, plants, and animals, and meet delightful people. Recently I went there with my youngest son and grandsons.

We closely examined beaver teeth marks on a large tree and talked about which way the tree might fall. It was a wonderful moment of togetherness there on our knees looking at those teeth marks.

It is not at all uncommon for me to be struck by some little thing and end up with the germ of a poem that I cannot get out of my head. The only solution is to scribble it down, warts and all. The following is an example of one such moment in time. It was inspired by seeing raindrops roll off the backs of ducks.

Mist over Shoveler's Pond

Today it is time to play
As raindrops fill the day.
The drops drift in from every place
And decorate all
    with a delicate grace.

The raindrops like diamonds
    gleam and shine
On ducks' backs all in a line.
Each diamond magnifies
    a feather bright
With the captured rainbow light.

The mist continues to fall;
As I walk I catch it all.
But I know it soon will end,
As on my way I wend.

University Slough, by Doug Schmitt

Cinnamon Teal, by Stuart MacKay

Trumpeter Swan, by Kathrine Lloyd

Western Sandpiper, by Dennis Paulson

Song Sparrow, by Alexandra MacKenzie

Red-winged Blackbird, by Doug Parrott

C. Birds of Montlake Fill

Because the Fill is probably the most intensely birded site in Washington, and because it serves as a habitat island in the middle of a big city, more rarities have been found here per acre than at any other site in the state. The following is a list of all the bird species seen at the Montlake Fill since recordkeeping began in the 1890s. It has been compiled with the help of numerous birders over the years (see list of contributors at the end). I wish to thank especially the people who kindly reviewed this record: Dennis Paulson, Tom Aversa, Evan Houston, Matt Bartels, Brett Wolfe, and Bob Vandenbosch. Despite the great care we have all taken to be complete and accurate, mistakes might have been made (as the politicians say). I encourage readers to contact me with additional sightings and/or corrections.

GREATER WHITE-FRONTED GOOSE   Uncommon winter resident. More common as migrant. High count of 27 on the Main Pond October 9, 2008 (*CSi*).

EMPEROR GOOSE   Rare visitor. One August 1988 (*KA*).

SNOW GOOSE   Rare winter resident and spring migrant. One reported wintering in the 1940s (*HL*). One wintered 1978 to 1979; one December 10, 1984 to March 6, 1985; one November 23 to December 9, 1987; one during April and first half of May 1989 (*KA*). One May 10, 1994 (*WOS/DMc*). One from February 2 to April 26, 2000 (*WOS/TAv*). One May 15 to 17, 2006 (*CSi*; *WOS/KAn, MiH*). One April 15, 2007 (*BtW*). High count: 200 flying over October 8, 2007 (*CSi*). Ten in December 2008; one January 1, 2009 (*CSi*).

BRANT   Rare visitor. One for half a day, late March 1986 (*KA*).

CACKLING GOOSE   Uncommon winter visitor and migrant, sometimes in large flocks.

CANADA GOOSE   Common resident and breeder.

MUTE SWAN   Occasional introduced resident and breeder. Three May 15, 1980; three September 29 and November 1, 1980; two December 11, 1980; two with young May 27, 1982; four December 27, 1982; one April 8, 1983; two with young June 11, 1983 (*ER*). Two attempted to nest, July 1989 (*CSi*). A pair with two young July 16, 1995 (*DP*). Latest sighting: one December 17, 1998 (*WOS/TAv*).

TRUMPETER SWAN   Rare winter visitor. Two flew over December 15, 1984 (*KA*). One October 16, 1998 (*BV*). Two November 5, 2007 (*WOS/NLr*). One November 10, 2007 (*WOS/JB*). Fifteen arrived December 22, 2008; eleven (eight adults, three immatures) stayed on the lake for months; the last two immatures were sighted March 5, 2009 (*CSi*).

TUNDRA SWAN   Rare winter visitor. Reported in the 1940s (*HL*). One late October through mid-November 1970 (*FK*). Three December 17, 1998 (*WOS/TAv*). One near shellhouse December 22, 2008 (*CSi*).

WOOD DUCK   Common (though sometimes reclusive) resident and breeder. Bred more commonly in the 1940s (*HL*), diminished after habitat loss, now common again as swampy woodlands increase. Unusual sighting: mother with nine babies May 28, 2006 (*CSi*).

GADWALL Common resident and breeder.

EURASIAN WIGEON Uncommon winter resident. Usually one or two present each year.

AMERICAN WIGEON Common winter resident, rare in summer.

AMERICAN BLACK DUCK Rare introduced visitor. One male from December 29, 1979 through June 10, 1980; one male November 7, 1981 (*ER*).

MALLARD Common resident and breeder.

BLUE-WINGED TEAL Regular spring and summer visitor.

CINNAMON TEAL Uncommon summer resident and rare breeder. Latest breeding record: mother with nine babies, summer 2009 (*CSi*). Occasional winter resident; one pair spent the winter of 2008-2009 (*CSi*).

NORTHERN SHOVELER Common winter resident and sometime summer breeder. Latest breeding record: mother with nine babies, summer 2009 (*CSi*).

NORTHERN PINTAIL Uncommon visitor, recorded every month (*ER, CSi*). Occasional winter resident in small numbers (*CSi*).

GREEN-WINGED TEAL Common winter resident, returning by late July (*BtW*). Occasional summer resident (*ER*). Eurasian subspecies (Common Teal) is a rare winter visitor: One between January 27 and April 27, 2000 (*CSi*). One January 4 to May 7, 2001 (*BV; WOS/TAv, JB*). One January 11, 2004 (*SMa*).

CANVASBACK Uncommon winter resident.

REDHEAD Found regularly in the fall (usually most common in November) during the early 1970s (*ER, DP*). Now uncommon visitor in winter or spring. Most recent record: one overwintered 2008-2009 (*CSi, EvH*).

TUFTED DUCK Rare visitor. One May 3, 1996 (*WOS/JHe*).

RING-NECKED DUCK Common winter resident.

GREATER SCAUP Uncommon winter resident.

LESSER SCAUP Common winter resident.

SURF SCOTER Rare visitor. One adult male February 11, 1980; one immature male October 7, 1980 (*MC*).

WHITE-WINGED SCOTER Rare visitor. Nine September 22, 1939 (*MC*).

LONG-TAILED DUCK Rare visitor. One March 26, 1981 (*ER*). One March 4, 1990 (*DP*). One October 29, 2006 (*WOS/JBr*).

BUFFLEHEAD Common winter resident. Occasionally one stays through the summer.

COMMON GOLDENEYE Uncommon winter resident and rare summer visitor. Two records for June: one in 1981, one in 1983 (*ER*).

BARROW'S GOLDENEYE Rare visitor. One January 21, 1981 (*ER*). Two April 25, 1988 (*KA*). One February 21, 2007 (*BtW*).

HOODED MERGANSER Common winter resident and uncommon summer breeder: Female with young in 1982 and 1983 (*ER*). One or two breeding females each year from 1985 to 1989 (*KA*). One juvenile July 30, 2006; female with young July 24, 2008 (*CSi*).

COMMON MERGANSER Uncommon winter resident and common spring migrant, as large numbers stage in the lake and bay before migrating.

RED-BREASTED MERGANSER Rare spring migrant. More common in the 1940s in the fall (*HL*). Five in April 1982 (*ER*). One April 15, 2008; two April 19, 2009 (*CSi*).

RUDDY DUCK Uncommon winter resident, formerly abundant: 500 January 1983 (*ER*). Rare summer visitor: one July 5 to 26, 1980; one August 19 to 29, 1980; three August 5, 1982; one August 12, 1982 (*ER*). Successful nesting 1987 through 1989 (*KA*). One July 25 through September 18, 2008 (*CSi*).

RING-NECKED PHEASANT Formerly common resident and breeder, now very scarce. Last reported: One vocalizing July 12, 2009 (*GOO*). One seen near Surber Grove July 21, 2009 (*MaH*).

CALIFORNIA QUAIL   Formerly common resident and breeder, now extirpated, although rare visitors still appear occasionally. One June 17, 2004 (*CSi*). One July 13, 2004; two July 29, 2004 (*BV*). One April 18 through the summer, 2007 (*CSi, BtW*). One April 14 and 15, 2008 (*CSi, WOS/TAv*). One April 8, 2009 (*DPa*). One calling May 5 through 9, 2009 (*CSi*).

NORTHERN BOBWHITE   Rare visitor. One September 11, 1997 (*WOS/TAv*).

COMMON LOON   Rare visitor. Reported regularly in the winter in the 1940s (*HL*). One fly-over July 16, 1980; one in Union Bay April 17, 1982 (*ER*). One flyover April 16, 2008 (*WOS/TAv*). One in Union Bay October 30, 2008 (*CSi*).

RED-THROATED LOON   One March 20,1943 (*ER*). Occasional winter visitor (*DP*).

PIED-BILLED GREBE   Common resident and breeder.

HORNED GREBE   Uncommon winter resident.

RED-NECKED GREBE   Rare visitor. One November 1979; one June 7, 1982 (*ER*). One September 4, 2007; one October 2, 2007; one December 1, 2007 (*BtW*). Two November 27, 2008 (*CSi*). Two December 23, 2008 (*EvH*). One February 14, 19, 21, 2009 (*EvH, CSi*). One March 13 and 29, 2009 (*EvH*).

EARED GREBE   Rare visitor. More common in the 1940s, arriving in fall (*HL*). Occasional winter visitor in 1970s (*FK*). One February 28, 1981 (*ER*). Two October 28, 1986; one September 18, 1989 (*KA*).

WESTERN GREBE   Uncommon winter visitor and migrant.

CLARK'S GREBE   Rare visitor. Two calling July 21, 1989 (*KA*).

DOUBLE-CRESTED CORMORANT   Common resident.

AMERICAN BITTERN   Former uncommon resident and breeder (*HL*), now scarce. Most recent sightings: One September 11, 2006 (*MtB*). One February 4, 2007; one October 5, 2007 (*BtW*). One July 25, 2008 (*CSi*). One July 7, 2009 (*KL*). Three August 8, 2009 (*DPa*). One August 19, 2009 (*CSi*).

GREAT BLUE HERON   Common resident and occasional breeder. Successful nesting in 1989 (*KA*).

GREAT EGRET   Rare visitor. One June 16 to July 2, 1987 (*KA*). Two May 15, 2000 (*WOS/RR*).

CATTLE EGRET   Rare late fall or winter visitor. One November 11 through 18, 2004 (*WOS/FB, KAn; MtB, CSi*). One November 5 through 9, 2007 (*BtW; WOS/NLr, CSi, CPe*).

GREEN HERON   Uncommon summer resident and breeder. First state nesting record, 1939 (*HL*).

BLACK-CROWNED NIGHT-HERON   Rare visitor. Two reported in the 1940s (*HL*). One December 5, 1974 (*FK*). One August 15 to September 3, 1987 (*KA*).

TURKEY VULTURE   Rare spring and fall migrant, only flyovers. One May 7, 1983 (*ER*). One October 3, 1985; one April 1, 1986; one November 4, 1987 (*KA*). One September 24, 1998 (*TAv*). One April 29, 2007 (*BtW, CSi*). Eighteen September 26, 2008; two April 8, 2009 (*CSi*).

OSPREY   Uncommon summer visitor. One or two come by regularly in summer and stay briefly to catch fish.

BALD EAGLE   Common resident and breeder. Current nest on Talaris site nearby.

NORTHERN HARRIER   Common visitor in the 1940s (*HL*). Several single records in 1980s (*ER*). In the 2000s, usually at least one seen each year, sometimes in winter or (more commonly) in fall. Most recent sightings: One May 16, 2008 (*MtB*). One July 30, 2008; August 13, 2008 (*CSi*). One October 5, 2008 (*WOS/EvH*). One May 6, 2009 (*EvH*). One August 12, 2009 (*CBB*).

SHARP-SHINNED HAWK   Occasional visitor, more common as fall migrant or in winter.

COOPER'S HAWK   Uncommon visitor, more common in fall and winter. One summered in 1985 and 1987 (*KA*). Three immatures in September 2008 (*CSi*).

NORTHERN GOSHAWK   Rare winter visitor. One February 3 and 19, 1972 (*FK*). Several sightings in winter of 1981 to 1982 (*ER*).

RED-SHOULDERED HAWK   Rare visitor. One August 7, 2006 (*CCx*).

RED-TAILED HAWK   One to three present in winter in years past. Pair became year-round resident in 2008 (*CSi*).

ROUGH-LEGGED HAWK   Rare visitor. Two flew over in late October 1974 (*KA*). One February 3, 1982 (*ER*).

AMERICAN KESTREL   Formerly regular fall visitor (*KA*), now rare. Twenty-seven records in the early 1980s (*ER*). One July 20, 2000; October 24, 2001 (*WOS/TAv*). One August 16, 2003 (*CSi*). Two August 21, 2003 (*WOS/TAv*). One August 12, 2007 (*CSi, WOS/JB*).

MERLIN   Occasional year-round visitor.

PEREGRINE FALCON   Occasional year-round visitor.

VIRGINIA RAIL   Uncommon summer resident and breeder in cattails. At least four nests in 2008 (*CSi*). Unusual habitat: one calling in Surber Grove March 22, 2009; two in same location March 23, 2009 (*CSi*).

SORA   Uncommon summer resident and breeder. Most recent sightings: Two July 21, 2000 (*CSi*). One September 12, 2002; one August 24, 2003 (*MtB*). One May 13, 2004 (*CSi*).

AMERICAN COOT   Common resident and rare breeder.

SANDHILL CRANE   Rare visitor, only flyovers. Two October 12, 1980 (*ER*). Three September 17, 2007 (*WOS/BtW*).

BLACK-BELLIED PLOVER   Regular migrant in 1940s (*HL*). Now rare. Two May 14, 1979; one May 5, 1980, one April 6 and 9, 1983; August 1 and 8, 1983; one first week of September 1983 (*ER*). One September 12, 1985 (*KA*). One April 22, 2004 (*WOS/EH*).

AMERICAN GOLDEN-PLOVER   Rare migrant. One September 14, 1981 (*DP*).

SEMIPALMATED PLOVER   Rare migrant. High count of five May 13, 1986 (*KA*). One May 31, 1996; one July 17, 1997 (*CM*). One August 6, 2000 (*WOS/JB*). Three August 7, 2000 (*CSi*). One April 29, 2007 (*WOS/PC, MEg*). One May 8, 2008 (*BV*).

KILLDEER   Common resident and breeder, though growing somewhat more scarce.

BLACK-NECKED STILT   Rare migrant. One May 12, 1988 (*KA*). One April 29, 1993 (*WOS/TB*).

AMERICAN AVOCET   Rare migrant. One May 28, 1980 (*ER*). One March 31, 1988 (*KA*). One May 30, 1998 (*WOS/BB*).

SPOTTED SANDPIPER   Uncommon resident and regular migrant. Bred commonly in the 1940s (*HL*) and annually in the 1970s (*KA*). Last reported nesting: 1987 (*KA*).

SOLITARY SANDPIPER   Rare spring and fall migrant; usually one present briefly each year.

GREATER YELLOWLEGS   Occasional spring migrant, uncommon fall migrant.

LESSER YELLOWLEGS   Occasional spring migrant, uncommon fall migrant.

UPLAND SANDPIPER   Rare migrant. One August 18, 1998 (*WOS/TAv*).

WHIMBREL   Rare visitor. One May 4, 1974 (*FK*). One in late September 1975 (*KA*). One May 3, 1981 (*ER*). One April 30, 1994 (*WOS/DMc*).

SANDERLING   Rare migrant. Two juveniles September 25, 1986 (*KA*).

SEMIPALMATED SANDPIPER   Formerly uncommon but regular fall migrant, now rare. Five spring records: One May 25, 1974 (*FK*). One May 13, 1976 (*DP*). One May 8, 1982 (*ER*). One May 10 to 12, 1996 (*CM; WOS/JiF*). One May 10, 2000 (*WOS/TAv*). Most recent fall records: One July 8, 2006 (*MtB*). One August 11 and 14, 2007 (*CSi, MtB*). Two August 12, 2007; one August 14, 2007 (*CSi*). One August 15 and 25, 2007 (*BtW*). One July 22, 2008 (*EvH*).

WESTERN SANDPIPER   Common spring and fall migrant.

LEAST SANDPIPER   Common spring and fall migrant. Rare winter visitor: one January 9, 1982; one February 5 through 9, 1982 (*ER*).

BAIRD'S SANDPIPER   Rare fall migrant, averaging one each season (*KA*). Highest count: three September 10, 1989 (*KA*). One spring record: May 9, 1985 (*KA*). Most recent sightings: August 14, 2007 (*CSi*); August 15 and 19, 2007 (*BtW*)

PECTORAL SANDPIPER   Rare spring and fall migrant, although usually at least one is present briefly each year. Slightly more common in fall than in spring. Most recent sightings: One July 22, 2008 (*EvH*). One May 15, 2009 (*CSi*).

SHARP-TAILED SANDPIPER Rare migrant. One September 29, 1996 (*WOS/KA*), last seen October 14, 1996 (*CM*).

DUNLIN Occasional winter visitor, occasional spring migrant. High count: more than 40, November 5, 2006 (*CSi*).

RUFF Rare visitor. One September 1, 1995 (*WOS/RSt*).

STILT SANDPIPER Rare visitor. One July 29, 1965 (*FK*). One August 30 to September 8, 1981 (*ER*). Two September 13, 1981 (*EH*). One August 29, 1989 (*KA*). One August 31 to September 1, 1996 (*CM, CSi*). One August 17 and 18, 1997 (*CM, BV*).

BUFF-BREASTED SANDPIPER Rare visitor. One stayed seven days, reported in the 1940s (*HL*).

SHORT-BILLED DOWITCHER Uncommon spring and fall migrant.

LONG-BILLED DOWITCHER Uncommon spring migrant, common fall migrant.

WILSON'S SNIPE Uncommon fall, winter, and spring resident.

WILSON'S PHALAROPE Uncommon spring migrant; usually at least one present each season. High counts: Four June 5, 2003 (*WOS/MtB*). One female, two males May 24, 2008 (*CSi*). One fall record: August 1, 1987 (*KA*).

RED-NECKED PHALAROPE Rare migrant. More common in the 1940s (*HL*). Sixty-five May 20, 1980; one August 7, 1980; one May 24, 1982; one July 22, 1982; one June 1, 1983; one August 9, 1983 (*ER*). One May 23, 1985; one August 23, 1989 (*KA*). One August 16, 1998 (*WOS/BB*). One September 5, 2005 (*WOS/JB*). One August 9, 2009 (*EvH*). One August 20, 2009 (*KL, JP*). Two August 21, 2009, remaining for some days (*CSi*).

BONAPARTE'S GULL Formerly common spring and fall migrant, now rare. Most recent sightings: One June 4, 2008 (*DPa*). One August 29, 2009 (*EvH*).

BLACK-HEADED GULL Rare visitor. One April 19, 1998 (*SMa, CSi*).

FRANKLIN'S GULL One reported in the 1940s (*HL*) for first county record. Occasional in fall (*DP*). Most recent sighting: one August 29, 2009 (*EvH*).

MEW GULL Common fall and winter visitor.

RING-BILLED GULL Common winter resident, less common in summer.

WESTERN GULL Rare visitor. One March 11, 1988 (*KA*). One January 21, 2009 (*CSi*). One February 11, 2009 (*EvH*).

CALIFORNIA GULL Uncommon fall and winter visitor. Most recent sightings: one February 2, 2009; one March 28, 2009 (*CSi*).

HERRING GULL Rare fall and winter visitor. One January 3, 2009; one March 17, 2009 (*CSi*).

THAYER'S GULL Rare winter visitor. One late, May 31, 1982 (*ER*). One October 28, 2007 (*BtW*). One November 5, 2008; one January 7, 2009 (*CSi*).

GLAUCOUS-WINGED GULL Common resident. Nested in summers of 1984 and 1985 (*ER*).

CASPIAN TERN Uncommon summer visitor, though present every summer.

BLACK TERN Rare visitor. One August 22, 1972 (*FK*). Two May 28, 1975; one late May 1976; one early June 1977 (*KA*). One June 8, 1980 (*ER*). One May 14, 2000 (*CSi*).

COMMON TERN Rare fall migrant. Eighteen August 19, 1980; two September 2, 1980; 25 September 13, 1982 (*ER*). Flock of 37 September 2, 1985; another flock of 26 September 3, 1989 (*KA*). Three September 10, 2003 (*WOS/SMa*).

ROCK PIGEON Common resident in University Village, commonly seen as flyovers and as foragers in playfields and in burns.

BAND-TAILED PIGEON Uncommon resident in the 1980s (*DP*), now uncommon visitor. Two August 22 and September 3, 2003 (*CSi*). One September 3, 2004 (*MtB*). One May 23, 2007; one October 28, 2007 (*BtW*). One May 19, 2008 (*MtB*). Two seen often in May 2009 (*CSi*).

EURASIAN COLLARED-DOVE Rare visitor. One May 10, 2008 (*CSi*). One April 18, 2009 (*GOO*). One April 20, 2009 (*CSi*).

MOURNING DOVE Uncommon visitor. Most recent sightings: One May 23, June 27, and October 23, 2007 (*BtW*). One July 6, 11, and 17, 2007 (*BV*). Two October 24, 2007; one May 24, 2008 (*CSi*). One seen off and on throughout July, August 2009 (*EvH, CSi, and many observers*).

BARN OWL Rare visitor. One October 1972 (*KA*). One September 4 and 16, 1980; one March 26, 1981; two May 4, 1981 (*ER*). One seen regularly in late July 2008 (*CSi*). One October 9, 2008 (*MtB*). One August 16, 2009 (*DPa*).

GREAT HORNED OWL Rare visitor. One March 18, 2007 (*MFM, CSi*). One November 7, 2007 (*MtB, TM*).

SNOWY OWL Rare visitor. Two wintered in 1973 to 1974 (*FK*). One seen in winter of 1975 to 1976 and 1977 to 1978 (*KA*). One March 3 to 9, 1979 (*ER*). One December 11, 2005 (*WOS/MtD*).

SHORT-EARED OWL Occasional visitor, now rare. One November 1992; one November 1995; one October 1996 (*BV*). One October 13, 1997 (*WOS/TAv*). One November 8, 1999 (*WOS/ED*). One October 19, 2006 (*BtW*). One November 25, 2006 (*WOS/TAv*). One January 17, 2007 (*BtW*). One November 13, 2008 (*EvH*).

NORTHERN SAW-WHET OWL Rare visitor. One October 14, 1995 (*WOS/PHa*).

COMMON NIGHTHAWK Rare migrant. Common summer resident in the 1940s (*HL*). Nesting reported in the early 1970s (*FK*). Now rare. One June 3, 1988 (*KA*). One September 20, 2002 (*WOS/SMa*). One August 27, 2004 (*WOS/SMa*). One September 18 and 19, 2006 (*WOS/PCr; EvH*). One June 8, 2008 (*MtB*).

COMMON POORWILL Rare visitor. One May 20 to 25, 2006 (*WOS/LKi, AdS*).

BLACK SWIFT Uncommon spring migrant and summer visitor.

VAUX'S SWIFT Common summer visitor.

ANNA'S HUMMINGBIRD None noted prior to the early 1980s (*ER, KA*). Now common resident and breeder.

RUFOUS HUMMINGBIRD Reported in summers in 1940s (*HL*). Rare visitor (*ER*) prior to the explosive growth of Himalayan Blackberry in the 1990s. Uncommon summer resident and breeder in the 1990s (*CSi*). Now much scarcer visitor. One July 11 through September 3, 2008; two June 22, 2009 (*CSi*). Single sightings in July and August 2009 (*CSi, EvH, and many observers*).

BELTED KINGFISHER Common resident.

LEWIS'S WOODPECKER Rare visitor. One September 3 to 10, 1984 (*ER*). One flying over August 25, 1987; one September 1, 1989 (*KA*).

RED-BREASTED SAPSUCKER Rare visitor. One early November 1982 (*ER*). One September 17, 1987 (*KA*). One December 5 and 9, 2007 (*BtW*). One March 25, 2009 (*EvH*).

DOWNY WOODPECKER Common resident and breeder.

HAIRY WOODPECKER Rare visitor. One calling (*HL*).

NORTHERN FLICKER Common resident and breeder. Occasionally, a yellow-shafted appears and contributes to the gene pool.

PILEATED WOODPECKER Rare visitor. One May 30 and 31, 2000 (*Tw/DWP*). Two July 14, 2002; one November 9, 2003 (*CSi*). One March 4, 2007 (*BtW, EvH*). One April 5 and 21, 2009 (*EvH*). One April 25, 2009 (*CSi*).

OLIVE-SIDED FLYCATCHER Rare visitor. One May 20, 1981 (*ER*). One August 27, 2003 (*WOS/TAv.*) One August 29, 2008 (*CSi*). One August 10, 2009 (*JeB, CSi*).

WESTERN WOOD-PEWEE Regular migrant.

WILLOW FLYCATCHER Common summer breeder in 1940s (*HL*). Now usually a visitor, most common in fall migration. However, three singing males in June 2009 (*CSi, EvH*).

LEAST FLYCATCHER Rare visitor. One August 17, 1998 (*WOS/KA*).

HAMMOND'S FLYCATCHER Rare migrant. One April 19, 2008; one May 2, 2009 (*CSi*). One May 8, 2009 (*EvH*).

GRAY FLYCATCHER   Rare visitor. One August 27, 2004 (*WOS/SMa*).

PACIFIC-SLOPE FLYCATCHER   Uncommon migrant.

SAY'S PHOEBE   Uncommon early spring or fall migrant. One late February 1977 (*KA*). One March 21, 1980; one March 28, 1982; one March 12, 1983 (*ER*). One September 18, 1986; one April 1, 1987 (*KA*). One October 3, 1994 (*WOS/DVi*). Two March 19, 1999 (*WOS/BB*). One March 11, 2004 (*WOS/MT*). One August 30, 2004 (*WOS/ST*). One or two each year thereafter.

ASH-THROATED FLYCATCHER   Rare visitor. One August 31, 1975 (*EH*). One August 31, 2009 (*CSi, KL*).

TROPICAL KINGBIRD   Rare visitor. One October 27, 2007 (*WOS/EH*).

WESTERN KINGBIRD   Uncommon spring or fall visitor. Most recent sightings: One May 22, 2003 (*MtB*). One September 1, 2003 (*WOS/JB*). One May 15, 2004 (*MtB*). One April 29, 2007 (*WOS/MEg*). One June 2, 2007 (*MtB*). Three April 22, 2009, two staying for several days (*CSi*). One May 13, 2009, remaining for at least two days after (*DPa, CSi*). One August 19, 2009 (*MBJ*).

EASTERN KINGBIRD   Rare visitor. One June 17 and 25, 1982; one July 6, 1982 (*ER*). One June 12, 1994 (*CPe*). One June 15, 1996 (*WOS/RR*). One August 9, 1997 (*WOS/TAv*). One June 7, 1998 (*WOS/BB*). One July 18, 1999 (*WOS/TAv*). One August 1, 1999 (*WOS/ST*). One May 29, 2005 (*WOS/TAv.*) One June 10, 2005 (*WOS/LrB*). Two June 19, 2005 (*WOS/DoM*). One May 29, 2006 (*CSi, MtB*).

SCISSOR-TAILED FLYCATCHER   Rare visitor. One August 2, 2003 (*WOS/SMa, CrM*).

LOGGERHEAD SHRIKE   Rare visitor. One May 25, 1975 (*DP*). One April 10, 1989 (*KA*). One March 31, 2004 (*WOS/DMv*). One April 12, 2008; one March 4 and 5, 2009 (*CSi*).

NORTHERN SHRIKE   Occurred regularly in October in the 1970s and 1980s (*KA*). Now uncommon winter visitor; usually one present each year. Most recent sighting: one November 14, 2008 (*CSi*).

CASSIN'S VIREO   Rare migrant. One May 1, 1981 (*ER*). One June 18, 1987 (*KA*). Flock on September 3, 2003; one September 5, 2004; one September 3, 2008; one May 23, 2009 (*CSi*).

BLUE-HEADED VIREO   Rare migrant. One September 8, 1995 (*WOS/KA*).

HUTTON'S VIREO   Rare visitor. One April 15 and 19, 2007 (*BtW*). One October 28, 2008 (*KL*).

WARBLING VIREO   Regular migrant in spring and fall in small numbers.

RED-EYED VIREO   Rare migrant. Four August 19, 1995 (*WOS/RR*). Two August 24, 1995 (*WOS/DB*). One August 22 and 29, 1996 (*WOS/KA*). One May 17, 2008 (*CSi*).

STELLER'S JAY   Common resident and breeder, reliably found in Surber Grove.

WESTERN SCRUB-JAY   Rare visitor. One September 24,1998 (*WOS/TAv*). One October 8, 2005 (*Tw/JBr*). One September 26, 2008, observed for a few days (*CSi*).

AMERICAN CROW   Common resident.

COMMON RAVEN   Rare visitor. One March 11, 2009 (*CSi*).

HORNED LARK   Scarce migrant (usually very late fall), seen one or two dates each year up to 2000s. Now rare. Most recent sightings: one December 4 and 5, 2005 (*MtB; WOS/TAv, JB, MiH*).

PURPLE MARTIN   Common summer visitor and fall migrant in the 1940s (*HL*) up to the 1970s (*KA*). Now rare migrant. Two September 3, 2003 (*CSi*). Six August 20, 2007 (*MtB*). Six August 29, 2007 (*BtW*). One October 5, 2008 (*WOS/EvH*). One August 12, 2009 (*EvH, GTh, CSi*); two seen later that day (*EvH*). One August 20, 2009 (*AdS*).

TREE SWALLOW   Common summer resident and breeder.

VIOLET-GREEN SWALLOW   Common summer resident and breeder.

NORTHERN ROUGH-WINGED SWALLOW   Uncommon migrant; a few seen every year.

BANK SWALLOW   Rare migrant. One May 30 through June 4, 1980; one September 4, 1980; one April 24, 1981 (*ER*). One August 21 and September 1, 1993 (*WOS/RTh*). One May 12, 1998 (*WOS/BB*). One August 9, 2003 (*WOS/SMa*). One May 11, 2004 (*WOS/SMa*). One

August 27, 2004; one March 19, 2008 (*CSi*).

CLIFF SWALLOW Common summer resident and breeder.

BARN SWALLOW Common summer resident and breeder; occasionally present in other seasons, though not as year-round resident.

BLACK-CAPPED CHICKADEE Common resident and breeder.

CHESTNUT-BACKED CHICKADEE Uncommon visitor. Most recent sighting: one March 6, 2009 (*EvH*).

BUSHTIT Common resident and breeder.

RED-BREASTED NUTHATCH Uncommon visitor; when seen, usually in Surber Grove. Most recent sightings: One January 6, 2007; one July 4, 2007 (*BtW*). One August 28, 2008 (*CSi*).

BROWN CREEPER Uncommon resident and breeder.

BEWICK'S WREN Common resident and breeder.

HOUSE WREN Rare visitor. One August 7, 2004; one August 18, 2007; one May 9, 2009 (*CSi*).

WINTER WREN Uncommon winter resident; most often found in Surber Grove and along the treeline south of CUH building.

MARSH WREN Common resident and breeder.

GOLDEN-CROWNED KINGLET Uncommon visitor, most often seen in winter and during migration.

RUBY-CROWNED KINGLET Common winter resident.

MOUNTAIN BLUEBIRD Rare visitor. One October 18,1984 (*ER*). One May 14, 1994 (*WOS/TP*). One September 28, 2007 (*WOS/MkW*). Two females April 3, 2009 (*CSi*).

SWAINSON'S THRUSH Uncommon summer resident in the 1940s (*HL*). Recorded most years in the 1970s and 1980s (*KA*). Now rare. Most recent sightings: One April 19, 2008 (*CSi*). One April 7, 2009 (*CSi, EvH*).

HERMIT THRUSH Uncommon migrant and winter resident. Most recent sightings: One April 30, 2008 (*MtB*). One May 2, 2008 (*EvH*). One April 20 and 21, 2009 (*CSi, EvH*). Two April 24 and 25, 2009 (*CSi*).

AMERICAN ROBIN Common resident and breeder.

VARIED THRUSH Rare visitor. One October 15, 1980 (*ER*). Most recent sightings: One January 5, 2007; one October 11, 2007 (*BtW*). One April 13, 2008; one April 18, 2009 (*CSi*).

NORTHERN MOCKINGBIRD Rare visitor. One October 28, 1993 (*WOS/KA, DB*).

SAGE THRASHER Rare visitor. One May 11 through 24, 2002 (*WOS/DP, CSi*).

EUROPEAN STARLING Common resident and breeder.

AMERICAN PIPIT Uncommon visitor. Most common in September, October, April, and May; sometimes overwinters. High count: more than 60, September 16, 2006 (*CSi*).

CEDAR WAXWING Common when fruit is available; nested in 2008 (*CSi*).

TENNESSEE WARBLER Rare migrant. One September 8, 1995 (*WOS/KA*) and again September 9 (*WOS/GT*). One August 19, 2009 (*CSi*).

ORANGE-CROWNED WARBLER Common migrant.

NASHVILLE WARBLER Rare migrant. One September 10, 1985 (*KA*). One September 25, 1994 (*WOS/DMc*). One September 10, 2005 (*WOS/TKL*). One September 30, 2005 (*WOS/KA*). One April 28, 2007; one April 26, 2008 (*CSi*). One May 10, 2008 (*EvH*). One May 12, 2008; one August 22, 2008 (*MtB*). One April 24, 2009 (*CSi*). One May 9, 2009 (*Seattle Audubon Board Birdathon*).

YELLOW WARBLER Formerly bred in small numbers (*KA*). Now only a common migrant.

YELLOW-RUMPED WARBLER Common migrant and winter resident. Both Myrtle and Audubon's present.

BLACK-THROATED GRAY WARBLER Uncommon migrant. Most recent sightings: One August 19, 2009 (*JeB, CSi*). One August 26, 2009 (*EvH, CSi*).

TOWNSEND'S WARBLER Uncommon migrant. Most recent sighting: one May 23, 2009 (*CSi*).

PALM WARBLER Rare visitor. One September 13 to 17, 1993 (*WOS/EN*). One September 20, 1998 (*WOS/BB*). One December 30, 2000 through April 15, 2001 (*WOS/RL and many observers*).

AMERICAN REDSTART Rare migrant. One August 26, 1988 (*KA*).

NORTHERN WATERTHRUSH Rare migrant. One August 17, 1989 (*KA*). One August 30, 1998 (*WOS/BV*). One August 21, 2003 (*WOS/TAv*).

MACGILLIVRAY'S WARBLER Rare migrant. One September 21, 1980; one April 30, 1981; one May 3, 1981; one May 18, 1982 (*ER*). One September 10, 1985; one August 16, 1989; one August 24, 1989 (*KA*). One August 24, 1995 (*WOS/DB*). One August 18, 1998 (*WOS/TAv*). One September 1998 (*BV*). One August 15, 2004 (*WOS/TAv*). One May 21 and 30, 2008; one June 4, 2008; one August 12, 2008 (*MtB*). One August 19, 2009 (*CSi, JeB*).

COMMON YELLOWTHROAT Common summer resident and breeder.

WILSON'S WARBLER Common migrant.

WESTERN TANAGER Uncommon spring and fall migrant, best found in Surber Grove.

SPOTTED TOWHEE Common resident and breeder.

AMERICAN TREE SPARROW Rare winter visitor. One January 11 and 15, 1981; one October 15 and November 7, 1981 (*ER*). One October 21, 1993 (*WOS/RTh*). One October 24, 2008; one February 21, 2009 (*CSi*). Formerly more common, averaging one or two a year (*KA*).

CHIPPING SPARROW Uncommon visitor. Most recent sightings: One April 28, 2007; three July 24, 2007 (*CSi*). One August 20, 2007 (*MtB*). One October 2, 2007; one November 18, 2007 (*BtW*). One August 3, 2008 (*CSi*). One April 7, 2009 (*EvH*). One April 14, 2009 (*CSi*).

CLAY-COLORED SPARROW Rare visitor. One November 7, 1999 (*CSi*). One April 28, 2008 (*MtB*). One September 5 and 6, 2008 (*WOS/JeB; CSi*).

BREWER'S SPARROW Rare visitor. One April 27, 1995 (*WOS/CH*). One September 22, 1998 (*WOS/TAv*).

VESPER SPARROW Rare visitor. One April 18, 1973 (*FK*). One May 8, 1976 (*KA*). One September 23 and 29, 1981 (*ER*). One September 5 to 12, 1985; one September 11, 1986 (*KA*). One April 29, 1996 (*WOS/MS*). One April 21, 1998 (*WOS/BB*). One September 24, 2002 (*WOS/MiH*). One September 1 to 10, 2005 (*WOS/KA, TKL*). One September 9, 2008 (*CSi*). One April 5, 2009 (*CSi*).

LARK SPARROW Rare visitor. One August 12, 2007 (*CSi*).

BLACK-THROATED SPARROW Rare visitor. One May 19, 1989 (*KA*).

SAGE SPARROW Rare visitor. One February 17 to 19, 1980 (*EH*).

SAVANNAH SPARROW Common summer resident and breeder.

FOX SPARROW Uncommon winter resident.

SONG SPARROW Common resident and breeder.

LINCOLN'S SPARROW Common winter resident.

SWAMP SPARROW Rare visitor. One November 20, 1987 (*KA*). One seen frequently from November 20 through December 24, 1995 (*WOS/DMc*). One April 14, 1996 (*WOS/DMc*). One April 5, 2005 (*WOS/ST, DnF*). One seen frequently in April 2008 (*CSi*).

WHITE-THROATED SPARROW Rare visitor. One October 4, 1981 (*ER*). One October 26, 1984 (*KA*). One October 7, 1993 (*WOS/RR*). One September 30, 1998 (*WOS/Tw*). One October 26, 2003 (*CSi*). One March 19, 2007 (*MtB*). One April 18 and 19, 2009 (*CSi*).

HARRIS'S SPARROW Rare visitor. One November 10, 1974 (*FK*). One November 1992 (*CSi*). One November 23 through December 18, 1993 (*WOS/LCo, RTh, DMc*).

WHITE-CROWNED SPARROW Common resident (mostly *gambellii* subspecies in winter) and summer breeder (*pugetensis* subspecies).

GOLDEN-CROWNED SPARROW Common winter resident.

DARK-EYED JUNCO Common winter resident, reliably found in Surber Grove.

LAPLAND LONGSPUR Regular fall migrant in 1980s (*KA*). Most recent sighting: October 6 through 18, 2007 (*WOS/BtW, MiH, MtB, CSi*).

CHESTNUT-COLLARED LONGSPUR Rare migrant. One December 3 through 12, 1995 (*MS, CSi, WOS/CM*).

SNOW BUNTING Rare visitor. One November 1975; one February 1976 (*KA*).

ROSE-BREASTED GROSBEAK Rare visitor. One June 1 and 3, 2003 (*WOS/RSh, MiD*).

BLACK-HEADED GROSBEAK Uncommon migrant and sometime summer visitor. Most recent sighting: flock of six, August 18, 2009 (*CSi*).

LAZULI BUNTING Rare visitor and breeder (evidence of breeding in 2008). One May 25, 1974 (*FK*). One June 29 and July 9, 1983 (*ER*). One August 19, 1988 (*KA*). One July 22, 1998 (*WOS/TAv*). One May 10, 2004 (*WOS/SMa*). One pair and possibly one other male, summer 2008; male first recorded June 1; immature recorded that year (*CSi, EvH*). Two males May 10, 2009 (*EvH*). A pair June 17, 2009 (*JeB*).

INDIGO BUNTING Rare visitor. One September 14, 1988 (*KA*).

BOBOLINK Rare visitor. One May 25, 1979; one June 2 and 3, 1980; one May 28, 1981; one September 3 and 14, 1981 (*EH*). One August 15, 1982; one October 10, 1983 (*ER*). One October 1 and 2, 1995 (*DP; WOS/BSu*).

RED-WINGED BLACKBIRD Common summer resident and breeder; also common as migrant.

WESTERN MEADOWLARK Former common summer resident in the 1940s (*HL*), now regular visitor in spring and fall. Three overwintered in 2008 (*CSi*) and one in 2009 (*CSi*).

YELLOW-HEADED BLACKBIRD Uncommon migrant. Most recent sightings: May 1, 2008 (*MtB*). June 2, 3, and 4, 2008 (*CSi, MtB*). April 28, 2009 (*CSi*).

RUSTY BLACKBIRD Rare visitor. One October 5 through 8, 1993 (*WOS/EN, KA*). One September 24, 1994 (*WOS/EN*). One October 31 to November 5, 1995 (*WOS/KA, EN*).

BREWER'S BLACKBIRD Common summer resident and breeder, with a colony recently established in the bushes around the helipad.

BROWN-HEADED COWBIRD Common summer resident and breeder.

BULLOCK'S ORIOLE Uncommon summer visitor and occasional summer resident. One pair nested in 1986. Most recent sighting: One pair May 22, 2006; one female June 21, 2006 (*CSi*). One May 1, 2008 (*MtB*). One June 4, 2009 (*EvH*).

GRAY-CROWNED ROSY-FINCH Rare visitor. Nine November 30, 1973 (*FK*).

PURPLE FINCH Occasional visitor, most often in migration but sometimes in other seasons. Most recent sightings: one September 23, 2008; one February 4 and 5, 2009 (*CSi*). Reported breeding, spring 2009 (*JeB*).

HOUSE FINCH Common resident and breeder.

RED CROSSBILL Rare visitor, usually flyover. One flock of fifteen May 2, 1985. Flock of eight, April 19, 2009 (*JeB*). Large flock April 22, 2009 (*EvH, CSi*).

COMMON REDPOLL Rare winter visitor. A flock of 28 on February 3, 1982 (*ER*).

PINE SISKIN Uncommon visitor in spring, fall, and winter.

AMERICAN GOLDFINCH Common resident, less common as a breeder.

EVENING GROSBEAK Uncommon visitor, usually flyover. Most recent sightings: Seven flying over and calling September 1, 2008 (*EvH*). One May 23, 2009 (*CSi*).

HOUSE SPARROW Uncommon resident and breeder. Most often found near Corporation Yard 3 in winter.

Observers

(listed alphabetically by last name)

KA Kevin Aanerud (note: most observations are from "Birds Observed at Montlake Fill, University of Washington Campus, Seattle, Washington, from 1972 to 1989" in *Washington Birds* 1: pp. 6-21, 1989; some observations are reports Kevin made to WOS since that date and are documented in WOS records); *KAn* Kathy Andrich; *TAv* Tom Aversa

JBr Jessie Barry; *MtB* Matt Bartels; *FB* Fred Bird; *BB* BirdBox (telephone hotline, published in *WOSNews)*; *TB* Thais Bock; *LrB* Lauren Braden; *JB* Jan Bragg; *JeB* Jeffrey Bryant; *DB* David Buckley; *CBB* Charlotte and Bill Byers

PCr Peter Carr; *LCo* Luke Cole; *CCx* Cameron Cox; *PC* Paul Cozens

ED Ed Deal; *MDo* Mike Donahue; *MiD* Michael Dossett; *MtD* Matt Dufort

MEg Mark Egge; *JiF* Jim Flynn; *DnF* Dan Froehlich

PHa Pete Hammill; *JHe* John Hebert; *HL* Harry W. Higman and Earl J. Larrison from their book, *Union Bay: The Life of a City Marsh* (University of Washington Press: 1951); *CH* Chris Hill; *MiH* Michael Hobbs; *MaH* Marc Hoffman; *EvH* Evan Houston; *EH* Eugene Hunn (note: observations are either Gene's personal records or observations noted in his book *Birding in Seattle and King County.* Seattle Audubon Society: 1982)

MBJ Melinda and Bruce Jones

LKi Lann Kittleson; *TKL* Tina Klein-Lebbink; *FK* Fayette Krause (from *Birds of the University of Washington Campus* by Fayette F. Krause (Seattle: Thomas Burke Memorial Washington State Museum, University of Washington, 1975)

NLr Norma Larson; *RL* Rachel Lawson; *KL* Kathrine Lloyd

DMc Dan MacDougall-Treacy; *SMa* Stuart MacKay; *TM* Tom Mansfield; *DoM* Douglas Marshal; *MFM* MaryFrances Mathis; *CM* Chris McInerny (note: most observations are from "Shorebird Passage at the Montlake Fill, University of Washington, Seattle, 1996-1997," in *Washington Birds* 8:19-28 (2002). Some observations are reports Chris made to WOS and are documented in WOS records); *DMv* Don McVay; *RyM* Ryan Merrill; *CrM* Craig Miller; *MC* Robert C. Miller and Elizabeth L. Curtis, "Birds of the University of Washington Campus," in *The Murrelet* 21:2, pp. 35-46 (May-August 1940)

EN Erica Norwood

GOO Grace and Ollie Oliver

DPa Doug Parrott; *DP* Dennis Paulson; *CPe* Curtis Pearson; *TP* Ted Peterson; *JP* John Puschock

ER Ellen S. Rattosh (from "Birds of the Montlake Fill, Seattle, Washington (1979-1983)," in *Washington Birds* 4, December 1995, pp. 1-34); *RR* Russell Rogers

AdS Adam Sedgely; *RSh* Ryan Shaw; *CSi* Constance Sidles; *MS* Mike Smith; *RSt* Rose Stogsdill; *BSu* Bob Sundstrom

MT Martha Taylor; *ST* Sam Terry; *GTh* Gregg Thompson; *RTh* Rob Thorn; *GT* Greg Toffic; *Tw* Tweeters

BV Bob Vandenbosch; *MVe* Mark Vernon; *DVi* Dick Viet

WOS Washington Ornithological Society (in "Washington Field Notes," published in *WOSNews* each issue); *MkW* Mike West; *DWP* Deborah Wisti-Peterson; *BtW* Brett Wolfe

Index